THE SINGLE-MINDED PRINCE

By
CARRIE STAPLES

THE SINGLE-MINDED PRINCE
Copyright © 2016 Caroline M. Staples

Contact Carrie Staples at:
Carrie@CarrieStaples.com
www.CarrieStaples.com

ISBN-13: 978-1530006694
ISBN-10: 1530006694

TABLE OF CONTENTS

THE BEGINNING

"His Majesty King Ollenfrond IX and Her Majesty Queen Tindra XII are pleased to announce the birth of their first son and heir, His Majesty Prince Bertram the First."

The commotion at the reception was thunderous. A few people were close enough to hear the Wizard Fernwake announce that Prince Bertram had been born under the Sign of Single-Mindedness. Nods of approval passed through the crowd. It was a powerful sign! No one considered it necessary to ask the Wizard for further clarification. Fernwake bowed and passed silently out of the great hall.

Gray Malkin, the Wizard's cat, slipped through the forest of feet to look at the new baby. He was very fond of children. It pleased him to see that Bertram was strong and happy. Only one thing puzzled him. He was convinced that the child was whistling. Newborn humans don't do that. Gray Malkin shook his head and followed the Wizard.

It didn't take long for others to notice that the Prince was whistling and chirping. The child devoted his energy to flapping his arms in a comical attempt to fly.

It was as if he were a bird trapped in a human body. He showed no interest in crawling or walking. There was no point in trying to bathe him in anything but a birdbath. The duck that played with the Prince in his bath finally convinced the child that legs could be a useful form of locomotion.

King Ollenfrond almost spilled his orange juice the morning his son waddled to the breakfast table. "This bird business has gone far enough," he roared at Bertram. "Stand up and walk properly!"

"Can't I ever waddle again?" asked Bertie, blinking back his tears.

"Waddling is considered excellent exercise," interrupted Queen Tindra. "It builds strong muscles." Bertie looked back at his father.

"You may waddle in your room," conceded the King.

The boy beamed and walked correctly to the table. He spent more time stuffing his pockets with breadcrumbs than eating his breakfast. He had a lot of birds to feed that morning. Soon he scrambled off to find his nurse. Some say she spoiled him even more than his mother did. As a founding member of the Royal Bird Society, she definitely encouraged his interest in birds.

One day, while the nurse and Queen Tindra were enjoying a cup of tea during their weekly conversations about Bertie, they hatched a marvelous idea. The Prince was always climbing the great tree in the courtyard to be closer to his beloved birds. He spent more time up in that tree than anywhere else. What he really needed was a nest!

Within a week the plans were drawn. The royal gardener explained to Bertie that his favorite courtyard tree would be off-limits for five days so it could be inspected for a possible unknown "condition". The tree was covered in billowing clouds of silk fabric. All day long and into the night, workers slipped in and out of the silk cover carrying an endless supply of peculiar items. Bertie watched impatiently from the castle window. He was concerned about his dear tree and hoped it would be okay.

Finally the royal gardener reported the tree was in excellent health and the silk fabric would be removed at noon that day.

Everyone but Bertie knew about the surprise so the courtyard was filled with people eager to watch the unveiling of the tree. As Bertie helped pull the silk down from the tree he noticed a strange shape near the top.

"What is that thing in the tree?" he asked.

"You'll have to climb up and examine it," answered the royal gardener. The excited crowd watched as Bertie climbed higher and higher. The birds that had been prevented from sitting in their tree for five days noticed the silk fabric was gone and they all started flying back to the tree. Bertie and the birds arrived at the great nest together. They were speechless for a moment. Then they all started to sing the happiest bird song ever sung.

From the nest Bertie looked out over the kingdom's peaceful green valleys full of more happy birds.

The shore and the sea and the sky were filled with even more happy birds. The morning moon smiled down upon them all, promising perfect balance and harmony from the raging winds of the world outside the happy kingdom.

Eventually Bertie looked down over the edge of his nest and remembered to thank everyone who had helped to create it. Queen Tindra and the nurse hugged each other happily. They soon realized it would not be easy to get Bertie to leave his nest for anything, and so, a set of Nest Rules had to be established. Dinner had to be eaten in the royal dining room with his human family, not in the nest. Bedtime meant going to bed in his royal bed in the castle, not in the nest. Oh dear…

Fortunately other things were also important to Bertie. Every day he and his nurse visited Professor Pockets, the Royal Bird Keeper. His son, Albert, was two-and-a-half, just like Bertie. The boys spent time playing hide-and-seek with all the unusual birds in the aviary. They practiced bird calls until they could mimic each bird. The birds soon forgot they were boys and sang along with them, laughing at the funny things the boys were singing.

The Royal Bird Keeper published an extensive study on the unusual relationship between the birds and the boys. It is out of print now, but Albert's great-great-great-great granddaughter has the original manuscript.

Bertram loved birds. There was no getting around it. He loved them almost as much as he loved his parents. There is nothing wrong with loving birds. Many people love birds. But it would not be an exaggeration to say nobody in the world loved birds more than Bertram.

Bertram's true love of birds made Ollenfrond uneasy. Although he was not sure why he felt that way, the King tried to keep Bertie's unusual love of birds a secret. He wished with all his might that no one else would find out about Bertie and the birds. But it was beyond even his royal control.

The extent of the leak became all the more obvious when Bertie opened his gifts at his third birthday party. He received the following:

137 rubber ducks
48 birdcalls
206 leather-bound bird books
79 singing canaries
526 white marble birdbaths
626 pink marble birdbaths
26 black marble birdbaths
12 jewel-encrusted gold bird cages
1002 assorted bird houses
17 filmstrips of birds in flight
2 plaster casts of bird claw prints
And too many china birds to count

Several other gifts probably got lost in the mountains of ribbons and paper. His favorite present was a ducky clock that quacked the hours. He learned how to tell time within a day.

Obviously Bertie's love of birds was not a secret. Ollenfrond's only official comment at the party had something to do with being glad that everyone knew how fond Bertie was of birds. Then he withdrew to his private quarters to spend the rest of the day in uninterrupted worry.

The welfare of the kingdom had to be considered. The crown could never be turned over to a peculiar prince, particularly when it was obvious that the entire world knew Bertram was peculiar. Why was the King so worried? The boy was only three years old. Ollenfrond tried to comfort himself with that thought.

THE BIRD KEEPER'S MISTAKE

After his fourth birthday, Bertie no longer spent time with his nurse. He preferred to go out on his own, usually to his nest, but he still visited the aviary every day. Professor Pockets, the bird keeper, was the most fascinating adult Bertie knew. He was an expert on the subject that interested Bertie most.

Sometimes Professor Pockets read to the boys from a great book called the *History of Birds*. They learned how different birds eat different foods and sleep in different kinds of places, how some birds like hot weather while others prefer cold. They examined pictures of beautiful birds living in distant lands. They learned that some birds have webbed feet for swimming and others have claws so they can scratch for or catch food.

One day a seemingly normal discussion with the professor turned Bertie's thinking in an unfortunate direction. Professor Pockets told the boys that cats are the natural enemy of birds. He explained that cats stalk birds to catch them and eat them for dinner. Bertie was horrified.

"There are cats living all around the castle," he cried. "Our birds are in terrible danger!"

"Oh, no," said the bird keeper, "Cats only eat birds when they are hungry. Cats must eat to live. Remember that birds eat worms when they are hungry and big birds eat mice and fish and other small creatures. You eat birds for dinner, too, just like cats. Our different eating habits are all part of the balance of nature."

Bertie had never thought about it before. His favorite chicken soup was made from a chicken!

"I will never eat a bird again as long as I live," he swore. "And I will have my father banish all cats from the kingdom immediately. I will protect birds from their enemies for as long as I live!"

"Me, too," said Albert.

"Let's consider the situation further before you make your decision," counseled the professor. He preferred not to suggest to the single-minded Prince that he might be wrong.

"We need cats," the professor continued, "They are our friends also. They keep mice from our kitchens and cold from our feet."

"The birds who like to eat mice could do that for us, and a wooly pair of socks is better than any cat," answered Bertie.

"There are big birds that don't live in houses. They make their homes on mountain tops with the earth far beneath them and the wide sky around them. They would not trade such freedom for a thatched roof and a smoky kitchen," explained the professor, hoping to make Bertie sympathize with the birds.

"Cats are different," he continued. "They like to make their homes in small, snug places behind the stove or among the pillows on somebody's bed. Cats have a long-standing agreement with humans. They keep a home free of mice. In return, people give them a warm, dry place to sleep and a bowl of cream."

"If I made friends with a large bird, he would keep mice out of my castle," answered Bertie, "especially if I promised him that he would never be bothered by cats again."

"That's right!" said Albert, who never had much to say because Bertie always said what he was thinking.

"Maybe you could get a bird to keep mice out of the castle if you tried very hard," said the professor, who understood the power of a determined boy. "But there are other things to consider. If all the cats were banished, birds would come from all over the world to live here. The balance of nature would be upset by an artificially created bird haven. Serious overcrowding would result. Such an imbalance would ultimately destroy itself."

"How could that happen?" asked the boys.

"Food would become increasingly scarce," explained the bird keeper.

"That's impossible," laughed the Prince, "Birds are so little there would always be enough food for them."

"It doesn't seem like they eat much now," said the bird keeper. "But suppose there are more baby birds than you can imagine. The food near the nests will be finished long before the babies are grown. Parents will be forced to fly far away to find food for their young. That will mean more work for birds that are already working very hard. The following year they may build their nests in a less congested location."

"That's an easy problem to solve," said Bertie smugly. "We'll feed the birds ourselves. My father can set up feeding stations throughout the kingdom."

"Your idea might work," said the professor. It made him uncomfortable to argue with the Prince. He was aware of the power Bertram commanded, even if the child was not. There was no point in continuing the discussion.

"Let's go make plans," said Bertie to Albert. The two ran happily off to the aviary. The Prince could create terrible problems if he had his way.

Professor Pockets hoped that King Ollenfrond could control his son. The boy had to be made to understand that what he wanted to do was wrong. Birds and cats had shared the same world for hundreds of thousands of years. There was no need for the change Bertram was planning.

A Learning Experience?

"My dear," said King Ollenfrond to his wife, "I have never heard such a strange request in all my life. Bertie wants me to banish cats from the kingdom. Why does he dislike cats so much?"

"Maybe he is allergic to them," suggested Queen Tindra, "just like I am."

"But you have nothing against cats," said the King.

"You are right. I admire them. They are truly beautiful and regal animals," said the Queen. "I have never said anything to encourage him to dislike cats. He has been brought up to love and respect all animals."

"I'm afraid he was born with his peculiar attitude toward cats," said the King, thinking about Bertie's upbringing. "Maybe our mistake was in allowing him to become so involved with birds. But I honestly can see nothing wrong with what we have done."

"We must give the boy an answer," interrupted the Queen. "We cannot banish all cats from the kingdom."

"Of course not," said the King, "but we cannot dismiss his request with a simple 'no'. He refuses to listen to reason on the subject of cats and birds. He must have an example from which to learn that he is making a mistake."

"What do you suggest?" asked the Queen.

"I will banish all cats from the castle. Bertie will see how unhappy the people are to give up their beloved cats. He will hear them complain of mice multiplying in the kitchens. And he will be able to compare life without cats inside the castle to life with cats outside," answered Ollenfrond. "If the boy is to become a good ruler he must realize that a king cannot be self-indulgent. The enforcement of rules based on unnecessary whims can turn the entire country against him. It will be a valuable lesson."

The following morning King Ollenfrond announced that all cats were banished from the palace. The Prince protested that his father's action was too weak. Ollenfrond told him that he would do no more and that Bertie had to be satisfied with the decision as it stood.

There was much grumbling among the people who lived within the palace. They knew about the young prince's request. Many of them felt that the King was spoiling his son, but Ollenfrond had always been good and wise. They comforted themselves with the thought that the King must certainly have a good reason for his action. Unhappily, they picked up their cats, tucked them in wicker baskets and carried them off to stay with relatives who lived outside the castle walls.

Everyone obeyed the rule except the Wizard Fernwake, who strongly doubted the wisdom of Ollenfrond's act. She warned the King in private that the decision to banish cats from the palace would hurt the Prince more than it would help him. The King was upset that Fernwake didn't agree with him, but he had given his word and he felt his decision was right.

"May you never regret this proclamation," Fernwake said quietly. She paused for a moment and continued, "It pains me to go against your edict, but I shall not allow you to banish Gray Malkin so easily from his home. If you wish to banish my cat then you must banish me also. I await your decision." The Wizard turned quickly to go.

"There is no need for you to leave," said the King. "Please ask Gray Malkin to remain always within your quarters. He will be safe there. Sending him away would be like sending you away. I cannot do it. I love you both too much."

The Wizard bowed and left without a word. The King felt the first pang of regret. He was afraid the Wizard was right. The cats were his loyal subjects also. He was treating them unfairly because of his son's whim.

CHICKEN POX

Bertie was miserable. He had chicken pox. The name of the disease bothered him twice as much as the condition itself. From his nest he dictated the following letter to the Royal College of Medicine:

Dear Doctors,

The royal person of Prince Bertram is extremely offended by the name of the illness he has been unfortunate enough to catch.

The entire kingdom must be aware of his young highness' deep affection for birds. It is therefore surprising that the Royal College of Medicine made such an error as to name a disease after a bird.

It is hoped that the error will be corrected immediately. The following list is hereby provided from which to select a more appropriate name:

Icky Pox
Purple Pimple Pox
Lima Bean Pox
Catchy Scratchies

Please notify his smaller highness of your decision no later than tomorrow morning. He does not wish to suffer from such a misnomer any longer.

Sincerely yours,
Prince Bertram I

The royal doctor recommended that Queen Tindra keep Bertie in bed and give him lots of orange juice and chicken soup. Then he remembered Bertie wouldn't eat chicken soup so he suggested beef broth instead. Then he remembered the boy would probably insist on spending his time recovering in his nest rather than in his bed.

What was a doctor to do? He left wondering how anyone could be as spoiled as Prince Bertie. If he continued to have his way, the child would turn into a very difficult king. Someone would have to talk to Ollenfrond, but the doctor wasn't up to taking on that responsibility himself.

The doctor didn't need to speak to the King. Ollenfrond was well aware of the problem. It was not just concern about his son that upset him. He was very fond of cats and missed having Gray Malkin and the other regular castle cats around. He was embarrassed to visit friends in the castle who had been forced to send their own cats away as a result of his edict. The length of their separation from their dear pets could now be counted in years.

Ollenfrond had comforted himself with the thought that Fernwake would solve the problem when she became Bertram's teacher. But his confidence was diminishing. Fernwake had refused to discuss the matter since the day Ollenfrond had banished cats. And that hadn't resolved anything. Bertram was campaigning harder than ever to have cats thrown out of the entire kingdom.

Ollenfrond had to speak to the Wizard privately. Could there be something seriously wrong with someone who thought of nothing but birds?

THE VISIT

Fernwake lived in a secluded tower at the southeast corner of the palace. A gnarled, old tree grew in the tiny courtyard at the top of the tower. Hidden deep within its leaves, Gray Malkin watched Ollenfrond approach.

As the King climbed the long, winding staircase to the Wizard's quarters he wondered how to bring up the subject. He might chuckle and say, "Funny how the Prince likes birds so much." Or maybe a less direct approach would be better. A greeting to Gray Malkin could lead to a line like, "Too bad the Prince doesn't appreciate cats." There had to be a way to bring up the subject so it didn't sound too serious. But he knew he would arrive at Fernwake's door long before he could figure out how to hide his feelings from his wise old friend.

Gray Malkin was at the great door to welcome the King. The Wizard came quickly down from her study to greet them.

"You're just in time for lunch," said Fernwake and she settled Ollenfrond comfortably at the table. The fire crackled as steaming bowls of contraband chicken soup appeared at each place.

"This is delicious," said Ollenfrond. "I haven't had chicken soup since Bertie realized it had chicken in it. I can't even have scrambled eggs for breakfast."

The conversation began and Ollenfrond poured out his concern. When Ollenfrond was through Fernwake shook her head.

"There is nothing we can do about Bertie's extraordinary love for birds. Being kind to them and protecting them are not bad things. Until Bertie's love becomes dangerous I am powerless to change it. We can only hope that as he grows up Bertie will develop other interests. For now we must be glad that he is a happy boy who is able to love."

"You always speak wisely," said Ollenfrond. "Your words comfort me." ·

Fernwake nodded. "You are a good king," she said, "and your

wife is a good queen. Goodness brings great reward. Your son will make you proud."

Gray Malkin and Fernwake walked the King to the door. The three friends said goodbye, happy to have shared an afternoon. The King felt renewed hope for his son.

As Fernwake watched Ollenfrond leave her face grew long and her eyes looked weary. She stooped to pet Gray Malkin and whispered in a magical language that only cats and wizards understand.

"l must share a terrible secret with you," Fernwake whispered, "I have searched the future for the fate of the young Prince. There is much darkness before there is light. In the darkness I could see nothing and I fear that it hid much sorrow. Then in the light I saw you as an old cat sleeping in the sunshine. There was a smile on your face. In the *Book of Visions* a smiling cat signifies peace, but what about the darkness?" sighed the Wizard. "What is it hiding?"

As Malkin listened his face grew long and his eyes looked weary too. He scratched his ear and then climbed to the highest branch of his tree to think about what Fernwake had told him.

Gray Malkin did not climb down until long after the Moon had set. The sadness of his fellow cats hung over him and he felt a frightening sense of responsibility. They were all there, outside the castle walls, waiting. They found the courage to live with the restrictions because of their faith in Ollenfrond.

Somewhere deep inside, Gray Malkin knew that the King was not destined to be their rescuer. Only a cat could save the cats.

Princess Timothy

Everyone in the castle rushed about with an increased sense of importance and anticipation. A baby was expected.

Bertie wasn't at all sure he wanted a baby except, of course, a baby bird. The excitement confused him and he felt left out. None of the preparations were for him. For the first time in his life he seemed to be in the way. He sulked in his nest and often took a sandwich up with him so he wouldn't have to come down until dinner.

The birds did their best to cheer up their friend, but it was useless. Even Bertie's mother was too busy for him, and that was a hurt the child couldn't bear.

It was not long before Bertie was informed that he had become a brother. He was completely unprepared for his new role. Suddenly he was supposed to be proud of his mother and proud of his sister and proud of himself. He could find no reason to feel proud.

At breakfast Aunt Mildawn talked about nothing but his beautiful baby sister. All he wanted to know was what had happened to his mother.

When he was finally allowed to visit her she said she was happy, but she looked very tired. Nobody else was worried that she was too weak to get out of bed except Bertie.

And then there was the matter of the 'beautiful' new baby.

When he saw her he was completely confused. She was red and she screamed. And she looked like a monkey. Princesses in storybooks were always pretty. How anyone could be proud of that funny-looking princess was a mystery to Bertie. Even his father had lost his mind. He said she was undoubtedly the most beautiful princess in the entire world. Bertie couldn't understand what had happened to everybody. He kissed his mother and ran out of the room.

When he reached the end of the hall he realized that nobody had followed him. They were too busy with the baby. He ran all the way to the aviary.

Professor Pockets and Albert were watching a mother bird sitting on her nest when Bertie arrived. They didn't even look at him.

"Be very quiet," cautioned the professor.

Bertie joined them and watched very carefully. The mother bird kept looking under her wing at a speckled egg.

"The egg is cracked," whispered Bertie. "Is it all right?"

"It certainly is," answered the professor.

They stood there as quietly as three mice. The egg wiggled and rocked. A piece of shell was knocked off by something inside the egg. Then a little beak poked out, followed by a tiny, floppy head. Before they knew it, the chick had gotten free of the shell and was snuggling up against its warm, fluffy mother hen.

"Its feathers are all yucky and sticky," said Bertie. "It looks funny."

"That's because it just came out of the egg. Soon all that sticky fuzz will dry and you'll be looking at the cutest, softest downy chick you ever saw," said the bird keeper. "All babies look funny when they are first born. It takes them a little while to start looking like we expect them to look."

"People babies, too?" asked Bertie.

"People babies, too," answered Professor Pockets. Bertie felt better. Maybe his sister would look okay in a little while.

He went to see his mother that afternoon, but he hardly had the patience to sit and talk. He had to check the cradle. His sister didn't look so bad after all, he thought. Maybe she really was the prettiest princess in the entire world, just like his father said.

"We are going to name her Timothy," his mother announced.

"That's a boy's name," said Bertie.

"Yes," answered his mother, "but we think it will be a good name for her. There are tall grasses that wave and dance in the wind called Timothy. They are so graceful and pretty with their lavender blossoms."

"Like a princess?" asked Bertie.

Queen Tindra nodded and smiled at him. Then she gave him a big hug. Bertie began to feel proud.

THE EDUCATION OF A
SINGLE-MINDED PRINCE

Bertie was pouring cocoa over his third cup of marshmallows when his mother arrived at the breakfast table.

"It certainly is a big day for you," said Queen Tindra, smiling at her son. "You must be very excited!"

Bertie nodded as he continued to slurp melted marshmallows. He and Albert and Professor Pockets were going to start training a peregrine falcon to hunt.

"I'm pleased to see how happy you are about your first day of school," continued the Queen. Three marshmallows stuck in Bertie's throat.

"But Mother," he cried, "I can't start school today. The professor is going to teach me how to train a falcon."

"It's been almost a week since your sixth birthday," said his mother. "You're not going to delay your education another day. Fernwake expects you at 8:30 this morning. You can learn to train a falcon some other time."

"I can learn school stuff some other time, too," answered Bertie angrily. "The falcon is ready to start training today."

"You are ready to start school and you are going to start today. There is no need for further discussion," said Queen Tindra. She began to eat her pink grapefruit.

Bertie knew he had lost the argument. It hadn't really been an argument. His mother had made the decision for him. She hadn't even bothered to ask him what he wanted to do. That must be what school is like, thought Bertie. They tell you what to do and you have to do it with no choice in the matter. He excused himself and walked slowly toward Fernwake's private quarters.

Gray Malkin and the Wizard watched his approach. Then the cat withdrew to the tower courtyard to hide in his tree.

The Wizard greeted Bertie with a warm smile. Bertie looked up at her out of the corner of his eye and didn't say a word.

Fernwake studied Bertie for a moment.

"What is bothering you so early in the morning, young man?" asked Fernwake.

"I was supposed to train a falcon today but my mother made me come to school instead," answered a very glum Bertie.

"That sounds fascinating," said Fernwake. "Let's go find Professor Pockets."

"Can we really?" Bertie asked, looking straight at Fernwake for the first time. Fernwake nodded and off they went.

That evening after supper King Ollenfrond turned to his son and said, "Tell me what you learned on your first day of school."

"Nothing, sir," answered Bertie.

"Nothing?" asked the King.

"Nothing that I would not have learned anyway," answered Bertie.

"Then what did you do?" asked Ollenfrond.

"Professor Pockets taught Albert and me the first steps in training a falcon to hunt," said Bertie.

"Didn't you see Fernwake?"

"She came along," answered Bertie. "But Professor Pockets was our teacher. I guess Fernwake doesn't know anything about how to train falcons."

King Ollenfrond looked at his son curiously. Fernwake had been Ollenfrond's teacher. He had respected the Wizard's wisdom for as long as he could remember. Bertie seemed to have a very peculiar attitude toward Fernwake. Ollenfrond was concerned.

The falcon's training continued every day for two weeks. Professor Pockets explained that training time varied from bird to bird. Although the falcon would require more daily workouts, the boys soon mastered the basic techniques.

Fernwake decided it was time to start regular classes. Bertie was to attend school six mornings a week and work with Professor Pockets during the afternoons. Bertie complained that he was not asked what he wanted to do. The next morning he growled at everyone at breakfast.

Bertie and the Wizard continued to have problems. Bertie wanted to learn to read from *Audubon's Book of Birds*, but Fernwake said the words were too hard for a beginning reader. Instead they read a book of stories about a prince his own age. Bertie thought the boy was dull. In one story the boy rescued a cat from a tall tree and Bertie hated him from then on.

Every night he looked in his *Book of Birds* to see if he could read it any better. He could pick out some words but it was a very difficult book. He realized that Fernwake was right about it being too hard, but he was still angry. It seemed that the Wizard ought to be able to wave a magic wand over Bertie's head so he could instantly read every word in the world.

Learning to read took so much time. Bertie was afraid he would be a hundred years old before he could read the *Book of Birds*. The idea of learning to read by magic interested Bertie. It seemed like an excellent plan. He asked Fernwake about it.

The Wizard said Bertie would never appreciate the ability to read if it was given to him with the wave of a wand. According to Fernwake, more magic came out of appreciation than came out of a wizard's wand. Bertie saw no logic in Fernwake's answer. The fastest, easiest way made the most sense. Maybe the Wizard wasn't as powerful as everyone seemed to think.

His father admired Fernwake's wisdom, but Bertie could not remember him talking about Fernwake's magic powers. As far as Bertie was concerned, everyone, including Fernwake, attached too much importance to the Wizard's words. Bertie wondered if her words really did have some special power.

Whenever Bertie and Ollenfrond had an argument about birds and cats his father would end the discussion by saying that Bertie would learn that Ollenfrond was right when Fernwake became his teacher. Bertie thought of Fernwake as a threat to his personal beliefs, an opponent who had to be defeated before she defeated Bertie. He feared they would never agree to disagree. And Bertie was not even a wizard!

Bertie suspected that words were the key. He was afraid that one day while he was listening to Fernwake talk in circles of wisdom, the Wizard would trick him into saying he liked cats. He worried that his belief would be magically weakened if he ever said that, even if he didn't realize what he was saying. He was determined to always be on guard against Fernwake's wisdom.

QUESTIONABLE DECISIONS

Bertie stared at the history books Fernwake had selected for him. He felt he was trapped at the bottom of the darkest prison. Why should anyone have the right to force him to study? He would sit and do nothing rather than open one of those dreadful books. His soul longed to escape. He imagined himself riding his swift ostrich across the countryside. They would never be captured.

Then Bertie had an idea. Maybe he could trick them all. He requested a private room in the library. The librarian was happy to comply. The room she selected was perfect for Bertie's plan. It had a large window opening directly onto the broad castle wall.

All he needed was a sign. The royal artist painted one for him, covered with swirls and furls and a wide golden border. Bertie carried it to his library room, hung it on the lion's head doorknob and closed the door behind him.

He sat down at his desk to watch the door, wondering if the sign would work. Just in case it didn't, he opened a fat history book so if anyone walked in they would think Bertie was studying.

After what seemed like hours he heard his mother talking to the librarian. Then he heard their footsteps coming closer and closer. Bertie held his breath.

"Oh, yes," the librarian was saying, "Bertie requested a private room."

"I am so glad," said Queen Tindra. "I was afraid he was going to be like his Uncle Clothfoote who has not opened a book since he was eight years old. And that was 43 years ago!"

By then they were right outside the study door. Bertie's heart was pounding. The voices that had been clear were suddenly very soft. Bertie listened hard to hear what they were saying.

"Look at the sign, Queen Tindra! 'DO NOT DISTURB! PRINCE BERTRAM STUDIES WITHIN'."

"How wonderful," whispered the Queen. "I certainly won't interrupt him now. When he comes out, please tell him that the cook has baked chocolate-chip cookies for his afternoon snack."

"That will be a nice surprise for such a hard-working boy," whispered the librarian. They tiptoed away.

Bertie almost shouted for joy. His sign had worked. He could do anything he wanted in his study! No one would bother him! Besides that, the cook had baked his favorite cookies. It was all he could do to keep from bursting out of the study and running to the kitchen. But the librarian would know he had been listening. He looked at the hourglass and decided to wait fifteen minutes so no one would be suspicious.

Fifteen minutes is a long time for someone to wait for chocolate-chip cookies. Bertie opened his window and climbed out onto the castle wall. An eagle on a mountain crag could not have felt a greater sense of freedom. Far below, the blue waters of the moat wrapped around the castle. Bertie could see beyond the distant mountain ranges. Tomorrow he planned to walk all around the castle wall. But for now his explorations would have to wait.

He closed the study window and ran to the door. As he opened it he remembered he wasn't supposed to know about the cookies. He walked casually over to the librarian's desk.

"Well," Bertie said, stretching and yawning, "all that studying certainly makes a fellow hungry."

"That reminds me," said the librarian, smiling at him, "there are chocolate-chip cookies waiting for you in the kitchen."

"Oh boy, what a great surprise!" exclaimed the Prince, as convincingly as possible. "I'll see you tomorrow," he called back as he raced toward the kitchen. He was amazed at how easy it was to fool people.

The next afternoon as he climbed out his study window onto the great castle wall, three sparrows and a pigeon flew over to greet him. They decided to play Follow-the-Leader. Bertie took the lead and started marching along the wall with regal dignity. The birds looked ridiculous trying to keep up with him. Bertie laughed and slowed down.

When he started to turn a somersault, Pigeon decided it was time for someone else to be leader and took over. He flapped his wings comfortably and flew above the castle wall with the Sparrows right behind him. Bertie flapped his arms as hard as he could and pretended to fly with them.

They were all laughing and having a wonderful time when Pigeon suddenly flew back to Bertie and clung to his shoulder. The Sparrows flew back, too. They were all extremely concerned about something.

"What is wrong?" asked Bertie. "There should be nothing in the castle to frighten you."

With the birds clinging nervously to his shoulders, he continued to walk along the wall. A gnarled, old tree grew from the tower ahead of him. He could not believe what he saw. On the highest branch of the tree a gray cat lay sleeping. The Prince was furious. He raced back to his study and charged through the library.

"Follow me!" he cried to a page as he ran toward the southeast corner of the castle. The sparrows, pigeon and page could barely keep up with him.

They came to a black walnut door whose sign read, 'The Wizard Fernwake's Private Chambers.' Bertie pushed through the door and raced up the staircase to the courtyard. He marched directly to the tree.

"Cat!" he cried. "I order you to come down from that tree immediately."

Gray Malkin woke from his nap with a start. He saw the Prince and the page below him and wondered what was happening.

"Cat," called the Prince. "I will not waste words on you. You must obey my orders and come down from that tree. You have broken the law and therefore you are my prisoner."

Gray Malkin was worried. The Wizard was away and he didn't know what to do about the intruders. He had always been taught to obey the royal family but he was afraid of the young Prince.

"Page," ordered the Prince, "shake the tree!"

The page was young and had not worked at the palace for very long. He knew nothing about Fernwake or her cat, and he could not imagine what the Prince was planning to do. He had to follow orders, but being kind-hearted, he shook the tree very gently.

"Shake the tree harder!" cried the Prince.

The page looked up at the cat and wished he would come down. But the cat was not moving and the page had to do what he was told. He shook the tree a tiny bit harder.

"No!" shouted the furious Prince. "You're not doing it right at all." Bertie ran to the tree and shook it with all his might.

Gray Malkin was not prepared for such a terrible attack and tumbled down through the branches to the hard brick walk below. He struggled to get up and escape, but he couldn't move. He had hurt his left front leg.

"Poor old cat," cried the page, rushing to pick up the wounded animal. He cradled Gray Malkin in his arms and whispered in the cat's ear. "I am so sorry. I did not understand. I will protect you from now on." He wished he could tell the Prince that he was very unkind but he was afraid to say a word.

"That cat deserves no sympathy. He has broken the Law," said the Prince. "Take him to the farthest edge of the kingdom and throw him out!"

"Yes, your Highness," answered the page. He wrapped Gray Malkin gently in his cloak and ran from the courtyard.

The Pigeon and Sparrows flew quickly to Bertie's shoulders.

"What a brave prince you are," chirped the birds. "You have conquered our enemy. We are grateful." Bertie could tell from their happy peeps that they were thanking him.

"It was the least I could do to help my good friends," answered Bertie, "Let's continue our game."

The Sparrows decided to be co-leaders and set off with Pigeon and Bertie behind them. In the confusion of having to follow three leaders at once the friends soon forgot about the cat.

The young page carried Gray Malkin quickly out of the palace. He was very much afraid that someone else would try to harm the cat.

"Brave cat," whispered the page, "Please trust me. I am Jonalon, the youngest page in the service of King Ollenfrond, but I cannot obey Prince Bertram's orders in spite of my position in the palace. He was wrong to hurt you. I will take you to Dr. Feather,"

In spite of the terrible pain in his leg, Gray Malkin purred to let Jonalon know he understood.

They were well into their second hour of walking when Jonalon and Gray Malkin arrived at Dr. Feather's door. Before Jonalon had a chance to knock, the door flew open. There stood a jolly, smiling man with a purring tiger cat draped over his shoulder.

DR. FEATHER

"Welcome Jonalon!" cried Dr. Feather. "Come in. And bring your gray friend. What good fortune brings you to my house? How are things at the castle? What is good old King Ollenfrond up to these days? Do you like the young prince? Why, there I go, asking you so many questions. One would think that if I asked a question I would have the courtesy to wait for an answer. I can see you have come on important business. Speak, boy, and don't let me interrupt."

"The gray cat has a wounded leg," said Jonalon. "Would you look at it, Sir?"

"Follow me," answered Dr. Feather. Away he went down a long corridor to a sunny kitchen where a friendly fire crackled in a fireplace half as big as the wall. The cook looked up from her kettle to smile at Jonalon, but Dr. Feather had already rushed ahead, out the kitchen door, and the boy had to run to catch up with him.

The doctor's office was on the other side of the herb garden. Jonalon, Gray Malkin and the tiger cat followed him inside.

"Now, gray cat," said Dr. Feather, lifting Gray Malkin carefully out of Jonalon's arms, "let me examine that leg."

Gray Malkin tried to hold his paw up, but it hurt so much he couldn't lift it.

"Poor Puss," sighed the doctor as he checked the hurt limb. "I'm afraid your leg is broken very badly. What an unfortunate accident." Dr. Feather wrapped Gray Malkin's leg carefully in gauze and plaster of Paris to make a strong cast. "You must take very good care of him while his leg heals."

"I can't do that, Sir," said Jonalon. "Cats are not allowed within the castle walls. What shall I do?"

"Let's go to the kitchen and discuss the problem there," said the doctor.

The table was set with tea and cream and sugar doughnuts. Dr.Feather placed a fat cushion on the table and helped Jonalon settle Gray Malkin comfortably on the pillow. Then he poured two cups of tea and two saucers of cream.

"There is nothing like a cup of tea and a saucer of cream to wash down problems. But I am being very rude! I have not introduced my fine tiger lady. Her name is Tuna-Una, short for the tuna fish sandwich I was eating when she found me. We shared that sandwich and have shared everything ever since! Now you must tell us how you and Gray Cat met," insisted the doctor. "Who found who?"

Jonalon related the unhappy tale. The doctor could not believe it. He turned to Gray Malkin and asked, "Could such a thing have happened to a gentle fellow like yourself?"

Gray Malkin nodded sadly.

"In that case you must stay here. Tuna-Una and I will be happy to take care of you. We three will get to know each other and we'll be able to count on more frequent visits from Jonalon. Please say yes."

Gray Malkin nodded his consent. There didn't seem to be any alternative. Dr. Feather and Tuna-Una were very nice. The Wizard would be extremely worried but what else could he do until his leg was strong enough to carry him home again?

"It appears that Gray Cat had a good home in the castle," Dr.Feather said thoughtfully. "You must tell that person about the accident. Give her our address. Assure her that we will take care of Gray Cat. When she comes here we will talk about where the cat should live."

Gray Malkin couldn't believe his ears. What a relief it was to know that Fernwake would be told soon. Gray Malkin felt much better.

Jonalon noticed that daylight was fading. "I must leave now," he said. "The King will be expecting me. Thank you so much for your help, Sir."

Dr. Feather picked up Gray Malkin. They all walked Jonalon to the door.

"Farewell my young friend," said Dr. Feather. "May the safety of sunny skies surround you. Please remember that we all wait impatiently for your return."

"Take care, brave cat," said Jonalon as he petted Gray Malkin.

"I will be back soon with news from your home. Good-bye everybody!"

Jonalon ran down the street. The windows in the town reflected the golden sunset. Tomorrow's problems were not far away. He was glad to have Dr. Feather for a friend.

JONALON AND THE WIZARD

Early the next morning Jonalon arrived at the Wizard's home. He stared at the sign on the great black walnut door for several minutes. He had never spoken to a wizard. The idea terrified him. But the gray cat needed his help. He knocked once, very lightly.

The door swung open as if by magic, though nothing odd appeared. Instead, he felt the safety of sunny skies surround him and he stepped across the threshold into an exciting new adventure.

Long before he reached the door at the top of the stairs it opened and a tall woman in a blue robe stared down at him.

"Good morning, Ma'am," said Jonalon. "I am Jonalon, a page in the service of King Ollenfrond. I have come with news of a gray cat."

"I am surprised to have a visitor so early in the morning," said Fernwake. "Most people who must visit me come late in the day. They spend many hours in fearful anticipation. When they finally arrive they are usually too frightened to speak. I tell them to write me a letter and I send them away."

"You come with unhappy news that will probably make me angry," she continued. "Yet you come bravely to tell your tale early in the morning. I like you for that. A problem presented in the morning is lucky because a whole day remains in which to find the solution. Tell me about my cat."

Jonalon retold the tale of Prince Bertram and Gray Malkin. He explained about Dr. Feather.

"Gray Malkin was fortunate to have found your friendship. I thank you. Will you come with me to visit them?"

"I would like that very much, Ma'am," said Jonalon, "but I must attend King Ollenfrond when the chimes strike nine this morning."

"We will be back in time," said Fernwake. "Follow me."

Jonalon wondered how it could be possible to visit Dr. Feather and return to the castle in less than an hour. But since Fernwake was a wizard, Jonalon was confident that what she said would somehow be true.

Fernwake took a dark cape from her closet. In the room the cape looked pale lavender. Jonalon was sure it had been dark gray in the closet. He watched curiously. As the Wizard carried the cape into the sunny courtyard it turned from lavender to pale blue and then to sky blue. The Wizard told Jonalon to stand directly behind her. Then she dropped the cape over herself and the boy.

A moment later she lifted the cape. They were standing on Dr. Feather's doorstep. Jonalon couldn't imagine how they had gotten there but he felt very special.

Dr. Feather answered Fernwake's knock.

"We are honored by your visit, Wizard Fernwake. Come right in," said Dr. Feather. "Good morning Jonalon. Now I understand what is so unusual about our gray house guest. We were just taking his breakfast up. He will be very pleased to see you. Come, Tuna-Una," he called. She rushed in from the kitchen and slipped quickly ahead of the group on the stairs. Jonalon thought he saw a large piece of bacon hanging from the side of her mouth.

Gray Malkin was just finishing the bacon when his visitors arrived. His tummy was full. Fernwake was there. All was well.

The group chatted happily. It was decided that Gray Malkin would stay with the doctor until his leg healed. Before they knew it an hour was almost over.

"Jonalon must return," said Fernwake. "And I have a serious matter to settle with the thoughtless Prince Bertram."

Everyone wondered what would happen when Fernwake and Bertie saw each other again. They were afraid for their Prince and angry with him all at once.

THE ENCOUNTER

Fernwake requested an audience with King Ollenfrond and Prince Bertram at noon that same day. The King, who was never too busy to see his friend, sent for the Prince. While the two waited for the boy, Fernwake told Ollenfrond what had happened.

Ollenfrond was puzzled.

"How could Bertie have been involved?" asked Ollenfrond. "He was studying in his room at the library when the accident took place."

"Jonalon seems like an honest and trustworthy lad," said Fernwake. "Although I sincerely hope Bertie had nothing to do with Gray Malkin's accident, I hesitate to doubt Jonalon. When did you see Bertie yesterday afternoon?"

"I didn't exactly see him," answered Ollenfrond slowly. "I stopped at his room in the library. He had a 'Do Not Disturb' sign on his door. Do you think he might not have been there at all? Could my son have been so dishonest?" Ollenfrond's chin sank deep into the palm of his hand. He stared out the window and saw nothing.

Fernwake did not speak. She knew the King wished to be alone with his thoughts. Soon Bertie arrived. "You summoned me, Father?" he asked.

"Yes, my son," answered King Ollenfrond. "The Wizard Fernwake has come to me with a tale which requires an immediate explanation. Tell me what you did yesterday afternoon."

"I had a great adventure, Father," answered Bertie without the slightest hesitation. "Last night you were busy so I could not tell you about it. Yesterday afternoon I found a cat on the palace grounds. I captured the cat myself and had a page take him to the farthest corner of the kingdom and throw him out. We will not be bothered by that wicked animal again," said the Prince proudly.

"Where did you find the cat?" asked Ollenfrond.

"He was hiding in the Wizard's courtyard," answered Bertie.

"Did you ask whose cat he was?" asked Ollenfrond.

"A cat can belong to a no one in the palace. They are illegal," said Bertie.

"Did you enter private quarters to capture the cat?" continued the King.

"There are no quarters in the palace which the Prince cannot enter," answered Bertie.

"You are incorrect in that assumption," said Ollenfrond. "There are no private quarters in the palace or elsewhere in all the world which any man can enter without an invitation. Do you enter my study before I have answered your knock?"

"No, Father."

"Do you interrupt your mother when she is working on her tapestry without asking her permission?"

"No, Father."

"Do you bother the cook in the kitchen if she has not first invited you to visit her?"

"No, Father."

"Then, by what right did you enter the private chambers of the Wizard Fernwake without first requesting permission?" asked Ollenfrond sternly.

Bertie was confused. He had expected praise for his brave deed. He could not understand why he was being interrogated. He looked at his father and Fernwake. Finally Bertie spoke.

"I did what I thought was right," he said bravely. He knew from the look on his father's face that the King did not agree.

"Was it right to cause a defenseless animal to fall from a high tree branch? When you knew the cat was hurt, was it right for you to have it taken to the far corner of the kingdom and thrown out? Should you not have taken the cat to a doctor for care? Did you not pity the animal at all? Do you still not regret your actions?" asked the King in an angry voice.

"No Sir, I do not," answered Bertie. "The cat is an evil creature that must be destroyed before he kills innocent birds."

"Your love for birds has gone too far," thundered the King. "If no one else can do it, I will make you learn to respect all living creatures! You will no longer have any choice in the matter."

The Wizard Fernwake stepped forward.

"Love can never be learned from an angry teacher," she said quietly. "Prince Bertram sees no wrong in his thoughtless act. He will not believe us when we say that it was wrong. He must learn the truth for himself. And he must learn it alone. I recommend that Prince Bertram's formal schooling cease. If there is something he wants to know he can find someone else to teach him about it. I will no longer decide for him what I think he should know. He has proved over and over again that he will learn only what he wants to know and nothing else. I hereby withdraw as his tutor. Life will teach him what I cannot."

Ollenfrond and Bertie looked at Fernwake in amazement. The Wizard bowed and departed. After what seemed like an eternity to Bertie his father turned to him.

"I will follow the Wizard's advice," said Ollenfrond slowly. "I have faith in her great wisdom. Yesterday you pretended to study in your room at the library, but you were elsewhere. You abused a privilege. Normally I would forbid you to ever use that room again, but the Wizard's words lead me to believe that should be your decision."

"It is a difficult task to learn everything for yourself," continued the King. "May good forces guide you quickly to manhood. Now Bertram, leave me before I lose myself in anger."

Bertie ran from the room. So much had happened so quickly that he wasn't sure what to think. Nothing could convince him that his attitude toward cats was wrong. Certainly Fernwake had tried everything to make him believe that cats were good creatures. Fernwake was wrong. And that was that.

But he had something else to think about. Fernwake had said she would no longer be Bertie's tutor. Bertie couldn't believe it! He never had to go to school again. The very idea made him jump for joy. In his glee he completely forgot about the bird-cat problem.

A child is rarely given the opportunity to educate himself. For a king's son to be in that position is rarer still. Young Bertie saw no need to do anything when Fernwake first withdrew as his teacher.

The King observed his son at play and wondered whether

Fernwake was right. He began to think that another tutor should be provided for Bertie. After considerable debate, Fernwake convinced Ollenfrond to let Bertie do as he pleased for one year.

"If his own natural curiosity has not driven him to seek sources of knowledge other than his own by then, Bertie should have a tutor to guide him," Fernwake counseled.

Ollenfrond was curious to see what his son would do under the circumstances. He accepted Fernwake's recommendation.

A New Adventure

Bertie spent most of each day in the huge nest observing activities in all parts of the kingdom with the aid of a powerful telescope. The view was spectacular from the top of the tree. He watched people going about their business from first light in the morning to the fall of complete darkness. Sometimes he watched until the last candle in the kingdom had been snuffed out.

It was fascinating. He saw fishing boats glide lightly across the sea in the morning and return slowly in the evening, riding low through the waves as they carried their cargo of fish to the docks. He learned to judge the size of the catch by how much of each boat showed above the water line. He noticed seagulls could always find as many fish as they needed even when the fishermen could not.

He observed battles between farmers and birds over possession of seeds. Even after the farmers had planted their seeds in the soil, the birds insisted on digging them up. He made a note to ask his father to outlaw scarecrows.

Shepherds spent hours searching for a lost lamb that a hawk could have found in a moment. Pigeons had to share the town squares with big, noisy horses that often forced the poor birds to take flight right in the middle of their lunch.

All the problems Bertie found interesting were related to birds. Fernwake's reading of the stars at Bertie's birth was correct. The boy had truly been born under the sign of single-mindedness.

Bertie's nest was the talk of the kingdom. The other children in the kingdom wanted nests of their own. It wasn't long before almost every child in the kingdom had one.

Realizing that all the other children wanted to possess what he already had, Bertie gained a greater understanding of his power. It would be easy to convince them to help him make life as easy and happy as possible for birds. After all, nobody could stop a king! He could hardly wait! He hoped his father would grow tired of ruling soon, and began to think about the tremendous control he would have as soon the kingdom was turned over to him.

Bertie realized that if he was really going to help all the birds, he would need a lot of help to prepare himself. He couldn't spend all his time studying birds. He had to learn to be a king so he could direct people to help him with his plans. He slid down from his tree and ran in search of Ollenfrond.

"Father," he called, as he rushed into the King's study. Ollenfrond looked up from his work.

"Father," continued Bertie, "you must teach me to be King! There are so many things a person should know if he is to be a good ruler."

Ollenfrond was overjoyed. After only a few months on his own, the boy understood he needed to be educated after all. Fernwake's idea had worked, "Certainly, son," he answered. "We can begin lessons immediately."

THE LIMP

For the first week after Gray Malkin's leg was broken there was nothing he could do except rest on his pillow. Tuna-Una visited him often. At night she purred to him until he fell asleep. Then she would curl up against him and gently wrap her tail around his hurt leg to protect it from things that go bump in the night.

Fernwake joined them for breakfast as often as she could. The Wizard's quarters seemed so empty without her dearest companion.

Gray Malkin missed the Wizard but he enjoyed staying with Tuna-Una and the doctor. Except for his hurt leg, it was like a vacation. Everyone took care of him and he was always the center of attention. By the end of the week he was happy to hear Dr. Feather say he could start walking. He had begun to grow tired of being so dependent on others.

At first he had trouble maintaining his balance on only three legs. He could not put any weight on his broken leg, but he became accustomed to the rocking, three-legged gait. Soon he could run through the garden almost as fast as Tuna-Una. He slept downstairs because it was difficult to climb. His first attempts had ended in failure and he felt very depressed. One evening Tuna-Una asked what was bothering him.

"I'm afraid I'll never be able to climb my old tree again."

"Of course you will," said Tuna-Una.

"I don't think so," answered Gray Malkin. "Every day I try the stairs. But I can only make it to the third or fourth step before I'm too tired to go on. And stairs are much easier to climb than a tree."

"When your cast is off it will be easier to walk again," comforted Tuna-Una.

"But what if I still limp after the cast is removed? What will I do with only three good legs?"

"Why don't you ask Dr. Feather?" said Tuna-Una. "There is no reason for you to continue to worry about an unanswered question when you know someone who can answer it."

"I'm afraid of what he will say," said Gray Malkin.

"You are afraid of knowing and afraid of not knowing," said Tuna-Una. Gray Malkin nodded. "Let's go find the doctor and put an end to this terrible waiting."

Dr. Feather was in his office studying cells under a microscope. When he looked up the cats were sitting right in front of him. "Dr. Feather," said Gray Malkin, "there is something I would like to ask."

"Obviously," said the doctor. "What can I do for you?"

"Will I ever be able to climb trees again?"

"I should think so," said the doctor.

"Do you know for sure?" asked Gray Malkin.

"No," answered Dr. Feather, "but don't devote too much of your time to worrying. The odds are in your favor. I once knew a cat with only three legs that had to give up climbing elm trees and restrict himself to apple trees. His condition was much more serious than yours."

"When will I know for sure?"

"Not for some time, I'm afraid," answered the doctor. "Next week we will remove your cast. But it will take several more weeks to recover the use of your muscles. All we can do is wait and see."

After what seemed like forever to Gray Malkin, Dr. Feather removed the cast. The cat carefully stretched his leg. It was so light without the cast that it felt like it was floating in the air. He lowered his leg slowly. Dr. Feather told Gray Malkin to put his paw on the ground and try to walk. The cat shook his head.

"If you don't try to use it, we can't see how well it has healed," said the doctor.

Gray Malkin put his paw gently on the ground and began to shift his weight to it. His knee buckled under him and he fell. Gray Malkin was frightened. He was afraid he couldn't walk. Not sure what to do next, he lay there, resting his chin on his paws.

"Don't worry, Gray Malkin. Your leg muscles are weak. In a few days they will grow stronger and your knee won't wobble as much," explained the doctor. "Please try to use that leg as much as you can to develop the muscles."

Gray Malkin sighed and stood up. If the doctor insisted, he

would try again. He held his leg as steady as he could and took a tiny step. This time he didn't fall over. But he limped very badly. He took another step and another. Everyone watched as he struggled to walk correctly.

"Poor Gray Malkin," each one thought to himself, "I hope his leg will be okay." A very worried Gray Malkin was hoping the same thing.

Three weeks later Dr. Feather met with Fernwake to discuss Gray Malkin's leg. Although it was much stronger, the cat continued to limp.

"Is there still a chance he will stop limping?" asked Fernwake.

"In time, exercise may reduce the limp to the point where it will be barely perceptible," answered Dr. Feather. "But you need not worry. Grey Malkin will be able to do everything he did before the accident. His ability to climb, which is so important to him, will be as good as it was. It may even improve because his hind legs will be stronger."

"Perhaps Gray Malkin would be safer living here with me and Tuna-Una," continued the doctor.

"If Prince Bertie ever gets his way, there won't be any place in the kingdom safe for cats," answered the Wizard. "I suspect that my quarters are as secure as any. Everyone knows Gray Malkin is no longer living with me. What do you think, Gray Malkin? The decision is yours."

Gray Malkin carefully jumped onto the Wizard's shoulder and licked her ear. Fernwake scratched Gray Malkin's head.

"My most loyal and trusted friend," said the Wizard. "Together we ... make a home for each other."

"Tuna-Una and I understand," said Dr. Feather. "But since we cannot visit you, we hope you will come here often."

"That will be our pleasure," answered the Wizard as she wrapped her cloak around herself and Gray Malkin. Dr. Feather was sure he heard someone say "thank you". But Fernwake and Gray Malkin were gone.

TIMOTHY'S DECISION

Timothy changed Bertie's life considerably. Before she was two years old, she made him realize that he couldn't just tell people what to do and expect them to do it. He had to convince her to do what he wanted. Every so often Timothy came up with a good suggestion. Instead of conceding that her idea was better than his, he would claim he was letting her have her way because she was his little sister. But now that she was four years old she was even more of a challenge.

Bertie and Timothy played and fought like all brothers and sisters. Only one thing divided them completely. Timothy loved birds but she refused to hate cats. She had seen a family of kittens once and had fallen in love with them. Even though he was eight years old, nothing Bertie said could convince her that cats were bad. They argued about cats endlessly. Finally Bertie realized that Timothy would never agree with him. They didn't talk about cats again.

One morning Bertie woke up dreaming of power. For a few sleepy minutes his whole soul longed for power. Then he realized he had nothing to worry about. Power was his birthright as the first-born son of a king. His mind soared, floating far above the kingdom. One day it would be his kingdom.

He could hardly wait to banish the cats. Timothy didn't approve of a kingdom devoted to birds. He wondered if she could interfere with his plans. People were always talking about the rights and responsibilities of a king, but no one ever discussed the role of a princess. At breakfast he asked his father what princesses are supposed to do.

"They're supposed to be graceful and gracious and good," answered Ollenfrond, smiling at his daughter.

Bertie glanced across the table at Timothy who was busy eating an orange and appeared not to be listening to the conversation. Except when they were fighting, she already was graceful and gracious and good. He had a feeling that she would be more than their father's description. She was very clever for such a little kid. Bertie wondered if she ever thought about power.

Timothy made up her mind during that breakfast conversation. It was boring to always be graceful and gracious and good. Learning to sew and draw and dance was fine, but she also wanted to learn to read and write and work with numbers.

After breakfast she bravely walked her four-year-old self to the far southeast corner of the castle to talk to the Wizard Fernwake.

She knocked and the door flew open. Inside the doorway stood a gray cat. They stared at each other in surprise for a moment. Then, without a word, Gray Malkin led Timothy up the stairs.

He tapped at a door. It opened and he walked in but she didn't follow him. Instead she waited at the doorstep. She looked all around until she finally saw Fernwake staring down at her from the balcony.

"Come in, Timothy," she called. "How wonderful to see you! Please tell me why you visit."

She took one step inside the door and stood there. "I don't want to be just graceful and gracious and good," she answered. "I want to be able to read and write and work with numbers. Will you teach me, please?"

Although the Wizard had never taught a princess, she couldn't see what difference it would make. If the little girl wanted to try, she was willing to help her. Besides, the Wizard was bored spending so much time with her own thoughts. Even though Bertie had been a problem, Fernwake missed hearing his ideas.

"We will start right away," announced Fernwake. "Come join me in my study. I have a book I think you will enjoy."

Timothy stopped to pet Gray Malkin before she climbed the stairs to join the Wizard.

"I see you and Bertie don't have the same attitude toward cats," said Fernwake. "I'm glad." She smiled at her.

"You must not tell anyone what I am doing," said Timothy. "I want to surprise my father and mother."

"You can trust me as I trust you with the secret of Gray Malkin," answered Fernwake solemnly. "Come sit beside me and I will introduce you to the mystery of words."

BERTIE'S ROYAL STUDIES

Ollenfrond created a series of lesson games. The first ones were easy. Bertie played the part of the king. Ollenfrond played his loyal subject. Ollenfrond would come before Bertie with imaginary wishes and complaints.

Pretending to be king was great fun. It increased Bertie's already large sense of power. Timothy complained that the games made Bertie impossible to live with. His natural bossiness increased every day. Ollenfrond assured her that the games would soon be much more challenging and Bertie would have less time to indulge in dreams of power.

The games did become more difficult. Instead of talking to loyal subjects, Bertie was confronted by foreign ministers. At first Ollenfrond pretended to be foreign ministers from friendly kingdoms. Bertie had to be careful to maintain good relations with them. It was extremely difficult to find ways to make friends with ministers from unfriendly kingdoms.

Ollenfrond gave Bertie many heavy, dusty old books bound in soft leather. The books recorded the foreign policies of their kingdom. They explained what Bertie's grandfather had done and what his great- grandfather had done before him and what his great-great-grandmother had done before them.

They all had problems with foreign countries which had to be resolved. Good solutions resulted in good friends. Sometimes solutions didn't work and anger would grow between the kingdoms involved. Foreign kingdoms might make unreasonable demands and refuse to consider a compromise. Bertie worked hard to find another way to solve those problems. He and his father argued about compromise. The boy felt it was wrong to compromise.

"If I am right and the other king is wrong," said Bertie, "he must do as I say."

"Who will decide which one of you is right?" asked Ollenfrond.

"I know I am right," answered Bertie.

"The other king may think that he is right," said Ollenfrond.

"Then he is lying," replied Bertie.

"Do I lie?" asked Ollenfrond.

"No, Sir," said Bertie.

"Then why do you argue and disagree with me?" asked Ollenfrond.

For a minute Bertie made no reply. He felt like he had been tricked by his father's questions. Ollenfrond interrupted his thoughts.

"You have not answered yet because no single, simple answer exists," he said. "If you are to become a just and fair king you must find a good answer to that question each time it appears.

"If one man says ice cream is bad for you and another man says ice cream is good for you, which man is right?" asked the King.

"The man who says ice cream is bad for you," sighed Bertie.

"Not necessarily," said Ollenfrond. "Both are right. Too much ice cream will give you a stomach- ache, but a reasonable amount is good for you. It has proteins and vitamins. Best of all, it is cool and smooth and tastes good."

"Is that a good reason to eat ice cream?" asked Bertie, "Because it makes you happy?"

"Certainly," answered Ollenfrond. "That's a good reason for doing a lot of things."

"It would make me happy to banish cats from the kingdom," said Bertie.

"Is your happiness worth so much unhappiness?" asked the King.

Bertie was about to answer when Ollenfrond interrupted him. "The lesson is over. You may present your answer to me in writing tomorrow."

THE SOCIETY OF BIRD LOVERS

Bertie's Society of Bird Lovers became the most active organization in the kingdom. Experts in all fields related to birds were invited to speak to the club. Experimental bird projects sprang up everywhere. The number of studies was endless. Volunteer birds did nothing but sit around and allow themselves to be cared for. Their feathers were preened. Their meals were prepared. Their homes were built. Their nests were tidied. Their claws were trimmed and polished. Their children were watched. They grew fat and lazy. And when it was observed that they were becoming fat and lazy, diets and exercises were prescribed. They didn't have to think for themselves at all.

Gray Malkin observed the activities from his tree.

"Except for the fact that cats aren't allowed to live within the castle walls," Gray Malkin confided to the Wizard one afternoon, "Bertie's Society has created a cat paradise. I've never seen so many plump, juicy and slow-moving birds in all my life. Some of them are so fat they've given up flying."

"You don't need to be warned," said the Wizard, "of what would happen if you got within sight of one of those birds."

"But there's no harm in daydreaming," answered Gray Malkin, smacking his lips thoughtfully. "After all, a cat is a cat. And to a cat, there is nothing like a bird, unless it's a fish," he said, smiling at his own obscure joke.

Fernwake shook her head. Sometimes Gray Malkin was impossible, and his sense of humor left something to be desired.

VACATION OPPORTUNITIES

Life in the kingdom continued in its normal, peaceful routine until the day a letter arrived by ship for Queen Tindra. It was an invitation to visit her sister, Queen Mildawn. The King hadn't had a vacation since before his 18th birthday. Queen Mildawn's invitation seemed like a perfect excuse.

"Besides," said Tindra, "Bertie is twelve. He is old enough to take on more serious responsibilities. A few weeks as acting king will teach him a lot. In such a short time he couldn't make any irreparable mistakes."

"You know," said Ollenfrond, "I think you're right. Let's do it! But before we make definite plans, let me discuss the matter with Fernwake."

The Wizard offered no opposition to Ollenfrond's idea. She had been watching Bertie and felt the boy had been taking the responsibility of studying to be king seriously. As long as the King left specific orders about what Bertie could and could not do, the Wizard felt it would be a valuable experience.

"I intend to leave you in the position of advisor," continued Ollenfrond. "If an emergency arises, allow Bertie to solve the problem if his plan sounds reasonable. I don't anticipate any difficulties. We will be away for no more than six weeks."

Bertie was very excited about being given the opportunity to be King. His father's instructions were reasonable except for one that stated specifically that no cats be banished during his father's absence.

Although Bertie did not like Fernwake, he knew his father had assigned her the job of advisor because no one else in the kingdom was better-qualified. The only question Bertie had after reading the instructions was, "When are you leaving?" Ollenfrond told him that preparations would take a month. It sounded like forever to Bertie.

"That month involves more than packing," said Ollenfrond, noting Bertie's frustration about the time, "We must also prepare you for your new responsibilities."

It hadn't occurred to Bertie that there was anything else he needed to know. Suddenly he realized what a tremendous responsibility he was about to undertake. More and more questions popped into his mind. He wasn't just going to be king of the children. Bertie had to govern the adults also.

Queen Tindra couldn't understand why Timothy didn't want to go with them to visit Aunt Mildawn. The princess hadn't been very active lately. Sometimes the Queen wondered what her daughter did all day long. Whenever she asked, Timothy would show her a tapestry she had been working on. Queen Tindra thought the work on the tapestry was proceeding very slowly, but she didn't say anything about it. It was a lovely piece of needlework.

Timothy told her mother she wanted to stay home to finish the tapestry in time for her father's birthday. Queen Tindra didn't think she could possibly finish it in six weeks, but it seemed like a good reason.

Actually Timothy was very worried about what Bertie might do while their parents were away. She had to stay home to watch him in case he threatened the cats.

Ollenfrond was disappointed that Timothy wasn't accompanying them. But when Tindra explained that she had something very important to do and winked he decided not to inquire further.

And so the ship was packed and preparations were completed. At the departure ceremony King Ollenfrond placed the royal robes of state on Prince Bertram's shoulders. The crowd cheered. Bertie felt very proud. He could barely keep from grinning.

Ollenfrond and Tindra kissed their children and climbed the ramp to the top deck. As they stood at the ship's rail waving goodbye, Ollenfrond frowned. "I wonder if I'm doing the right thing," he said.

"Keep smiling and waving," answered Tindra. "We are taking a long overdue and well-deserved vacation. Let's enjoy our six weeks of freedom."

Ollenfrond decided she was right. Suddenly a big smile broke out on his face and he hugged Tindra and said, "Can you believe it?

We're on vacation!" Before long it seemed as if the ocean had washed the land away. The ship was surrounded by sparkling blue waves that carried them gently toward Queen Mildawn's island kingdom.

THE GREEN GOULDRED

The waves were also carrying them directly into the path of another ship, the Green Gouldred, whose captain, Brute Nastie, was the most feared and terrible pirate king in the history of the entire world. The mention of his name made stout-hearted and strong-stomached sailors immediately seasick. At the sight of the Green Gouldred's sails, ships actually turned around and headed in the opposite direction without waiting for the helmsman to steer them.

As much as sailors feared Brute Nastie, the unfortunate passengers of a ship about to be plundered feared his first mate, Gangplank. Rumors of Gangplank's terrible deeds were said to have reached all the way to the Moon.

Some shrugged and said, "Why worry? After all, they are only rumors."

But that was what was so terrible. The tales remained rumors because no one whose ship was captured by the Green Gouldred ever returned to tell his story.

One sunny morning when the breeze was so gentle that it barely lifted the corner of a silk scarf, Ollenfrond and Tindra sat dozing on the deck. Ollenfrond could not remember a vacation he had enjoyed more. Suddenly a drop of water fell on the King's forehead. He opened one eye to examine the sky. There wasn't a cloud to be seen. He sighed with relief. It wasn't raining.

It also occurred to him that it couldn't be salt spray because the ship wasn't moving fast enough. But directly above Ollenfrond, the captain was leaning over the railing, crying like a baby and showering the King with his tears. When the King asked what was wrong he cried even louder.

Ollenfrond scanned the horizon and immediately saw what was bothering the captain. They were heading directly toward a galley with black sails. A Green Gouldred was emblazoned on the mainsail. The ship was riding swiftly across the water under the power of its oarsmen. There was no escape as their own ship depended on wind for power and the wind was resting.

As Ollenfrond watched the oars on the pirate ship rise and fall he shuddered. It was rumored that those whose lives were spared by Brute Nastie spent the rest of their days manning the oars in the dark belly of his pirate ship.

"Oh dear, oh dear, oh dear, oh dear," moaned the captain.

"Send up the welcoming flags. Move all the tables to the main deck for a buffet and set a small table for four on the sun deck," said the King, giving orders so fast that even the captain followed them without thinking.

"Have the crew dress in their best uniforms and hang all the bunting," called the King as he hurried down the stairs. He stopped just long enough to tell Tindra they were expecting guests and to dress accordingly. Then he headed down to the kitchen to talk to the chef about the brunch menu.

The crew was so shocked by all the preparations and activity that they forgot to worry about the terrible fate about to descend upon them. The ship's musicians tuned their instruments while one ingenious sailor covered the gangplank with red carpet.

Trays of hot breads and muffins, sausages and scrambled eggs, bacon and ham steaks, creamed smoked finnan haddie and eggs Benedict streamed out of the galley, followed by pitchers of fresh orange juice, pots of steaming coffee and rich cocoa, followed by butters, jams, honeys and syrups in dozens of tiny pots, followed by stacks of pancakes and French toast and waffles to be served with sugar and clotted cream. It all smelled so delicious that everyone began to hope the pirate ship would arrive before the food got cold.

Gangplank reported to Brute Nastie that the ship they were approaching was flying flags of greeting. A little later he reported that wonderful smells were wafting toward them. Nastie had also been studying the strange activities on board the ship through his telescope when suddenly his nose twitched.

"Creamed smoked finnan haddie," he sighed dramatically. "Creamed smoked finnan haddie is my favorite food in all the world." Turning to Gangplank he said, "Order the oarsmen to pull harder! We must reach that ship before they eat up all the finnan haddie."

Ollenfrond noticed a burst of speed in the pirate ship as he set a bottle of champagne in a bucket of ice next to the table for four. Tindra was busy dipping fresh strawberries in powdered sugar and arranging them artistically on cut-glass plates.

Soon the Green Gouldred drew alongside. Out of habit, the band struck up a chorus of "God Save the King" as the red-carpeted gangplank was dropped into place.

Brute Nastie, who had been planning to charge over the gangplank waving his sword and killing anyone who stood between him and the finnan haddie, was so flattered to hear "God Save the King" being played for him that he put his sword back in its scabbard and strode with dignity across the gangplank to the other ship.

"It is a pleasure to welcome the renowned and respected Brute Nastie aboard our ship," said Ollenfrond, bowing correctly.

"I have heard so much about you," said Tindra. She smiled and extended her hand to be kissed. Before she had time to wonder if her husband had lost his mind, the pirate king bent and kissed her hand. The crew of the Green Gouldred had never seen their captain act in such a strange manner.

"You and your crew must stay and have brunch with us," Ollenfrond continued calmly. "I am sure there is enough for everyone."

Brute Nastie suddenly remembered the finnan haddie and he began to feel evil again. "I am not so sure about that," he growled. Tindra thought she was going to faint. "How much finnan haddie is there?"

Ollenfrond led him to the buffet table and lifted the cover from a huge golden platter. There in front of Captain Nastie lay more creamed smoked finnan haddie than he had seen in his entire life. "As long as that dish is reserved for me," he said to Ollenfrond, "we will accept your invitation."

Ollenfrond signaled for the cabin boy to take the platter to their private table. Captain Nastie followed the boy to make sure he knew where he was taking the finnan haddie. Then he returned to the main deck and called to his crew, "A sumptuous repast has been prepared for us. Come and enjoy the hospitality of our hosts."

Nastie's crew was starving by then. They quickly put up their swords and raced to the banquet tables on the main deck.

The crew of Ollenfrond's ship was so excited to find themselves alive after being tied up next to the pirate ship for nearly ten minutes that they felt like celebrating also. Ollenfrond, Tindra, Capt. Nastie, and the captain of Ollenfrond's ship retired to the private deck while their crews sat down together and began to feast and enjoy themselves.

As soon as the champagne was poured Ollenfrond stood up. "I would like to propose a toast," he said, lifting his glass. Tindra was so nervous and confused that she started to pass the cinnamon toast. Ollenfrond glanced at her. She put down the tray of toast and picked up her glass.

"To chance meetings on the open sea and to their chances of friendship," continued Ollenfrond. They all drank. Brute Nastie suppressed an appreciative laugh and the terrified captain almost choked on his tongue. Then they all started eating strawberries.

The silence was overwhelming. Soon the berries were gone and the main course was served. Tindra was frantically trying to think of something light and insignificant to say to get the conversation started.

"What a handsome mustache you have," she said to Captain Nastie. He wore his blond moustache in ringlets and it was rumored that he tied the ringlets back with pink ribbons to keep them out of his soup.

"Why thank you, Madame," he answered, and pulling two pink ribbons out of his breast pocket, he tied his moustache back. Tindra blanched. At least one of the rumors was true!

"I find my moustache a bother when I eat. Otherwise it is very useful. It prevents anyone from knowing if I am smiling or frowning. The element of surprise is so much fun," he continued, smiling so broadly that Tindra could count his teeth.

Ollenfrond wondered what they might discuss after Captain Nastie had finished the finnan haddie. "How have things been going in your business?" Ollenfrond finally asked.

"I would prefer not to discuss business while I am eating," answered Nastie. Ollenfrond sat quietly wondering what kind of business they would discuss after Captain Nastie had finished the finnan haddie.

Queen Tindra was wondering if everyone could hear her swallowing. The poor ship's captain was wondering how much longer he had to live. And Brute Nastie was wondering how finnan haddie could taste so good. In less time than everyone had hoped, Nastie had finished the entire golden platter of fish. He called the cabin boy to his side.

"Young man," he said, removing one of the pink ribbons from his mustache, "please offer my compliments to the chef and tell him that as long as he continues to prepare such delicious finnan haddie for me his life will be long and prosperous. Also ask him to wear this pink ribbon prominently displayed in his hair. It will prevent my men from making any tragic mistakes."

The boy scampered down the stairs as fast as he could. Tindra tried to remember if she had any pink ribbons packed in her trunks. Brute Nastie sat back and sipped coffee through the side of his mouth that was still exposed. His cold eyes looked piercingly at each of his hosts.

"It's such a lovely day," said Tindra.

"Yes," answered the terrified captain, "Yes it certainly is. It is a lovely day. I can't remember such a lovely day. No, I certainly can't. I really don't believe I can. Come to think of it, it is probably the most beautiful day I have ever seen. Yes, it certainly is."

Queen Tindra was frantically trying to think of a way to change the conversation again. It was obvious that the captain could continue in the same vein for another hour at least. She interrupted him. "Tell me, Captain Nastie," she said, "how you acquired such a love for finnan haddie." Ollenfrond smiled at her. It seemed like a perfectly peaceful subject.

"I will be glad to tell you," he said. "When I was a poor starving orphan of six miserable years I washed icky stickystuff out of the bottoms of old bottles in a workhouse for a rich man. He then filled those bottles with colored water and sold them to destitute mothers as tonic for their children's ails. Every noon the restaurant across the street delivered a steaming dish of creamed smoked finnan haddie to him. The aroma permeated the air as we sat in the basement below him eating stale cracker crumbs soaked in dishwater. I swore that one day I would have all the finnan haddie I wanted and a basement full of rich men who lived on nothing but stale cracker crumbs and soapy dishwater." He paused and looked around at his audience.

"It's such a beautiful day," he continued with half a smile showing. "Why do you all look seasick? Maybe it is because you didn't like my story. That's too bad. Maybe it's because you began to see yourselves as characters in my story. Of course that must be it. You recognize yourselves as the rich men. But, I don't have a basement so why should you worry? Isn't that so?" They all nodded and tried to smile.

"No. It certainly is not so!" shouted Capt. Nastie, banging his fist on the table so hard the deck shook. "My basement is now below deck in the cargo hold. It is there that the men who were once rich now sweat and strain to support the poor they once robbed. And you shall join them!"

Ollenfrond stood up and refilled the champagne glasses. He didn't look at all concerned. "You must collect a great deal of loot," said Ollenfrond.

"I certainly do," answered Nastie.

"As your ship grows heavy with treasure, I suppose it must be harder for your oarsmen to row fast enough to catch other ships," continued Ollenfrond.

"That is true. We must stop often to bury our plunder. And that hurts," continued Capt. Nastie. "We see many ships full of riches we must pass by because our hold is too full."

"I can understand how that might distress you. What a terrible injustice it is for a wealthy ship to escape your clutches just because you are overweight," said Ollenfrond.

"What are you trying to say?" asked Nastie curiously.

"It is possible you could use another ship on which to store your plunder. Then the Green Gouldred would be light and ready to attack at all times," suggested Ollenfrond.

"That is a very interesting idea," said Nastie. "I could use another ship and crew for that purpose. But what good would a king and queen be to me?"

"What does a man miss most at sea, but the sense of hearth and home and pleasant conversation that a woman provides?" said Ollenfrond simply. "As for me, every man must discover for himself of what value a king can be to him."

Brute Nastie removed the other pink ribbon from his moustache. "There are points to consider in what you have said," commented Nastie. "I can see from your actions this morning that you are a clever man. Therefore, on a trial basis, you and your wife will stay with me aboard the Green Gouldred. With you as my prisoners, I am sure your loyal captain will not leave my side. We will try your suggestion of a second ship. Right now it saves us the bother of having to unload your goods onto our ship."

CHALLENGES

And so King Ollenfrond and Queen Tindra became prisoners of the terrible Captain Brute Nastie with no bloodshed and a minimum of ill will. Their new quarters were small but sufficient. They had all their meals with Captain Nastie and in a short time they became friends.

As Ollenfrond wandered around the ship he observed the crew at work. He made suggestions to Nastie about how to increase efficiency.

Queen Tindra passed her time creating a tapestry of the Green Gouldred attacking a fat merchant ship. Nastie liked the tapestry immensely.

They might have enjoyed the excitement and adventure of life on a pirate ship except for one problem. Prince Bertie was not prepared to rule over a long period of time. When Ollenfrond asked if he might send a message to his kingdom, Nastie just laughed and lived up to his name.

Meanwhile, Queen Mildawn was wondering where Tindra and her husband were. She sent a ship to inquire. When Bertie received the message that his parents had never reached their destination he became extremely worried. He sent his Royal Navy to search for them. He wanted to lead the search, but Fernwake counseled him to remain at home. The kingdom was his primary responsibility.

The boy suddenly realized what that meant. For the first time in his life he looked at ruling as more than a game. He didn't feel ready to be a king and he hoped his parents were found soon.

Weeks passed and unsuccessful ships returned only to be sent out again and again. It was a year before Bertie called the last ship home and ended the search.

On his fourteenth birthday Bertie was crowned King. As he marched toward the throne he looked very solemn and serious. But as soon as he felt the weight of the crown on his head he grinned from ear to ear. He continued to smile through the rest of the ceremony.

Before the day was over, King Bertram The First's Society of Bird Lovers swung into action. Cats were banished from the kingdom. A National Bird Year was declared. People who had cats realized there was nothing to do except ship their pets off to live with relatives in other kingdoms. Society members began an intensive search for illegal cats. Gray Malkin and Fernwake went immediately to Dr. Feather's house.

"Gray Malkin and I feel that it would be safer for Tuna-Una to live with us," said the Wizard.

"I suppose you are right," sighed the doctor, hugging his beloved Tuna-Una. "If I try to hide her here, they are sure to insist on a search. It would be terrible if they found her. If she is with you, at least I will be able to see her often."

Dr. Feather helped Tuna-Una pack her belongings. They all seemed to lose their voices when it was time to say goodbye.

BIRD POWER

To this day no one has been able to give a clear explanation of what happened next. Somehow the kingdom was turned over completely to the birds. Carrier pigeons flew to all corners of the world to announce that there was now a kingdom free of cats where all birds were welcome.

Bertie was unprepared for the incredible response. Birds began to arrive immediately. Each day flocks flew in from farther away. Exotic foreign birds appeared which weren't even listed in *Audubon's Book of Birds*.

It was an exciting time for the Bird Lovers Society. When people woke to the sound of bird songs, they could no longer say, "Listen to that robin in our maple tree." In the same tree where one robin used to sing, there might be 40 different birds. It often took hours of thumbing through bird books to identify them.

The newspaper had a special section to inform people about birds not listed in any available books. It was fascinating to learn who all the new arrivals were but soon enough some of the adults began to be more excited about seeing an old friend like a blue jay or a chickadee or maybe an evening grosbeak.

Every day Bertie met with flock leaders from newly arrived delegations. They sat in the King's huge nest and ate popcorn. A committee of parrots who had learned to speak English (somewhat rudely) on various ships around the world, interviewed each bird leader to determine what kinds of food, housing and recreation his group preferred. The parrots reported to Bertie who then directed other committees to fill those requirements.

At first the birds were surprised by all the attention. It was difficult to stop expecting to find a cat lurking around the next corner. But it didn't take long to adjust to their new position in society. The freedom from cats was exhilarating. Having their meals provided was a luxury they quickly took for granted. They each spent about an hour a week addressing members of the Bird Lovers

Society. The rest of their time was devoted to leisure activities.

The birdbaths were extremely popular. No bird was too busy to stop off to splash around and gossip for a few hours a day. The baths became overcrowded. Larger baths were installed in every square and smaller ones appeared on every street corner. When a delegation of human mothers came to request a swimming pool for their children, Bertie made a royal proclamation that children should use the birdbaths so they could become acquainted with their new neighbors.

Almost immediately the birds complained to their parrot spokesbirds that children created a disturbance at the baths. Bertie rescinded his proclamation. The mothers set up a grievance committee. Fernwake reminded Bertie that he needed the support all of the people in the kingdom. Bertie wasn't the least bit concerned.

"After all," he told Fernwake, "every one of those children is a member of the Bird Lovers Society. They certainly would not want a swimming pool built for them until the birds have all they need. We are committed to caring for birds."

Fernwake returned to her quarters. There was no way to talk to Bertram of the Single Mind, as more were beginning to call the young King in private.

Department store windows displayed bird fashions. Birds discovered the fun of shopping. Fish markets, which had suffered a mild setback after cats were banished, found their business was bigger than ever. As more birds stopped flying, buses added roosts over the seats to accommodate them.

Before long all the trees and building eaves in the kingdom were full and could hold no more nests or birdhouses. A committee was established to find new locations. When they realized that the only reason birds wanted to live above the ground was to avoid cats, they thought their problems were solved.

Within the week, little houses appeared on everybody's lawns. Some people preferred to construct bird apartments because it was difficult to keep the grass trimmed around row after row of tiny individual homes.

The problem of feeding all the birds soon seemed insurmountable. Within six weeks of Bertram's coronation every citizen had to dig worms for three hours before breakfast and one hour before dinner. The adults had been grumbling for several weeks when the children began to lose patience also. A protest delegation carried an ultimatum to King Bertie that read, 'The birds must feed themselves or leave!'

Bertie was aware of the growing unrest. He had scientists working around the clock to find a way to efficiently raise enough worms. Luck was on Bertie's side. They solved the problem on the morning Bertie was to meet the protest committee. When they arrived, Bertie greeted them with a big smile. "Guess what?" he said happily. "All worm-digging will stop permanently on Monday."

They weren't sure they heard him correctly. They yawned and tugged their ears. Finally one voice piped up. "Monday?" she asked.

"That's right," answered Bertie. "Unfortunately it will take that long to implement the new system. Only 15 people will be needed to run the new worm-raising program. Five carts can distribute worms to feeding stations throughout the kingdom. The birds will be able to pick up worms at their own convenience."

A cheer rose from the protest group. People waiting outside to learn the results of the discussion heard the cheer and passed the message along. Soon everyone in the kingdom learned they were free of the dreaded digging. The birds celebrated too because they still didn't have to dig for worms.

Fernwake often wondered how Bertie could be so lucky. Every time a conflict arose between birds and people something prevented it from becoming serious. The general welfare of the kingdom received little attention, but Ollenfrond had left the affairs of state in excellent shape before going on vacation.

Bertie had other unusually good luck. His merchant ships often met pirates on the high seas. For some unknown reason the pirates gave them no trouble. So Bertie was spared yet another problem.

Unfortunately the inconveniences people had to endure grew steadily. A new disaster occurred one morning when a very large man stepped on a very small bird. The man felt the bird under his foot and picked his foot up rapidly. Little damage had been done, but the birds immediately sent parrot representatives to the King to complain about careless people and their gigantic feet.

Bertie met with representatives from both sides. The people insisted that it was ridiculous to expect them to watch out for little birds wherever they went. "After all," said one person, "there's more to look at in this world than the ground."

Bertie realized that was a valid point. If a person had to watch the ground all the time he would have to learn to recognize his friends by their feet. And something wonderful like a sunset could only be seen through a carefully held mirror. It would not do to require people to watch the ground all the time.

"Another problem is the kind of weapon a person chooses to wear on his feet," squawked a parrot spokesbird with an eye patch. "By not covering our claws, our feet are sensitive. People wear thick leather soles and pointed heels and toes. If they step on something they don't feel it, but we certainly do! They also ignore signs like 'Keep off the grass' and 'Cross at the green.' So many people jaywalk that jays have started using crosswalks to avoid being stepped on. It's not fair!"

The people and birds stood there with their arms and wings crossed and glared at each other.

"Both sides have strong arguments," said Bertie thoughtfully, "but I believe we can find a solution. People cannot always watch the ground. Therefore birds must make themselves more obvious. Small birds will wear tall head feathers from now on when they are walking in populated areas. Shoes can be dangerous weapons on the wrong feet. Since it is impossible to predetermine who has careless feet, people will henceforth go barefoot or wear very soft shoes." The parrots quickly translated his message.

People feared shoe designers would complain and birds thought tiny birds might have trouble balancing extremely long feathers on their heads. They finally agreed to try Bertie's suggestions. People discovered the joy of soft shoes with low heels and little birds felt very special wearing long feathers on their heads. Favorable comments were heard about the wisdom of King Bertram the

Single-minded. Even Fernwake was impressed by how well Bertie solved problems.

BACK ON THE GREEN GOULDRED

Another year passed and Ollenfrond and Tindra continued to sail with Brute Nastie. They secretly dropped messages in bottles into the vast ocean. But they saw little hope and made the best of their situation. Tindra was happily designing a series of tapestries that related Nastie's entire life history. Ollenfrond, who had started out as Nastie's bookkeeper, was now his business manager. His new career began when he offered to keep a complete record of all treasure captured by the Green Gouldred.

One day he pointed out to Nastie that burying treasure was a waste of time and money. "Treasure planted in the ground doesn't grow," Ollenfrond counseled. "But treasure invested multiplies."

Nastie couldn't believe there was a way to turn treasure into more treasure. He considered treasure the final product of all business ventures. Once you had it, you had it, and that was that. It's not as if a gold dish could have baby gold dishes…

Ollenfrond plotted out a series of ways to invest Nastie's treasure profitably. "I will make a wager with you," Ollenfrond challenged Nastie. "If you dig up your treasure and invest it, you will end up with more money than you get plundering merchant ships. You could retire right now and let your money work for you."

"Do you mean I could make more money not working than I make working?" asked the amazed pirate. He felt like laughing at the idea. But in the time he had known Ollenfrond he had learned to appreciate the cleverness of the King.

"Don't hold out on me," Brute growled, hoping that the slightly threatening sound in his voice would make Ollenfrond work out his ideas faster. Brute was not a man who could stand suspense.

"What if I don't want to retire?" Brute continued. "I enjoy being a pirate captain."

"Isn't there anything in the world you like better than being a pirate captain?" asked Ollenfrond.

Brute closed his eyes and smiled. "Finnan haddie," he sighed, hardly able to keep from drooling. "But let's not waste time worrying about what I would do instead."

Ollenfrond showed Brute sheets and sheets of figures to explain how an investment would work. "You might as well invest in the area you know best," said Ollenfrond, "foreign trade. For three diamond-studded crowns you could provide a good man with a ship, crew and cargo. He could trade the cargo for goods needed in his own country. When he sells those goods at home he will make a sizeable profit. Most of that profit would go to you because you provided all the money for the venture in the first place."

"But I make more money now," said Brute, feeling like Ollenfrond had let him down. "I steal all the cargo on a ship and it doesn't cost me anything."

"True," answered Ollenfrond. "But what if you outfitted ten ships or twenty or even fifty? What would you say about the profits under those circumstances?"

Nastie smiled at the thought. Then he frowned. "You think you are so clever," scowled Nastie. "Try to outsmart me, will you? I shall have your head for that suggestion!"

Ollenfrond turned white. He had no idea what Nastie was talking about.

"Try to get me sent to the gallows, will you?" roared Nastie. "Don't you think I know what would happen if I set foot on land with all my treasure? How long would I be a free man?"

"There ought to be a way to invest your money without anyone knowing whose money it is or where it came from," answered Ollenfrond calmly, relieved to know what was bothering Nastie.

"Yes," said Nastie, as he began to think positively about the suggestion again. "You could handle all my investments in disguise. Of course Gangplank would have to go with you to make sure you don't escape."

"As long as Gangplank wears civilian clothes, that condition is completely agreeable to me," answered Ollenfrond.

"Then it's done!" said Brute, smiling happily at the thought of making even more money. "How long will I have to wait before I see my profits?"

"It will be at least a year before you see the results of your investments," answered Ollenfrond.

"I refuse to wait that long," said Nastie. "You'll have to work out a quicker investment."

"Quick investments are more uncertain," explained the King. "There are many more ways to lose money in an overnight deal than in a carefully planned, longer-term investment."

"Do you really think your idea will work'?" asked Nastie.

"If I didn't have considerable faith in it I would never have presented it to you," said Ollenfrond. "Think of the consequences I might face if I failed. Who knows what you would do to me in your anger."

"True," said Nastie thoughtfully. "My terrible anger must always be considered. Since you believe so strongly in this investment scheme that you are able to overcome your extreme and justifiable fear of me, I am willing to give it a try. We shall sail to Seaworthy Harbor in the Kingdom of Wooldown immediately."

The black sails of the Green Gouldred were replaced by plain white canvas. The crew was required to wear red and white striped jerseys and navy trousers instead of their normal casual pirate attire. Everybody got a haircut. Nastie trimmed his beloved but infamous moustache. And poor Gangplank was forced to spend his days getting comfortable in civilian clothes and shoes. The crew could barely control their laughter as he teetered by in fashionable but extremely *un*comfortable high-heeled boots. When lace collars replaced his neck chains, their sides practically split. Gangplank, who felt more miserable and embarrassed than he had in his entire life, started to blush. At the sight of Gangplank blushing, the members of the crew could no longer control themselves. They laughed right out loud.

Within a week the Green Gouldred, newly re-named the Snow White Swan, sailed quietly into Seaworthy Harbor. As Nastie looked around at all the fat merchant ships anchored there he could barely contain himself. "Let's forget about the investment idea," he suggested to Ollenfrond. "I could steal as much here in a day as those investments could bring home in a year."

"That is probably true," answered Ollenfrond. "But it is time for you to start planning ahead. If you attack these ships, all the important harbors in the world would hear about it and fortify themselves. Even if you changed your disguise they would catch you soon enough. The decision is yours. Will you plunder today and destroy the cover that allowed you to sail freely into the harbor to conduct legitimate business? If you do, you will never be able to sail safely into another harbor to invest your money. Instead you will have to spend the rest of your days robbing merchant vessels until your ship sails into a trap and you are caught and hanged."

Nastie listened intently as the King elaborated. "Today you can take the first steps toward preparing for a quiet retirement full of grandchildren who will marvel at your tales of life on the high seas. Can't you sacrifice a single day of plundering to help prepare for a peaceful future for yourself and your crew?" Nodding in assent, Nastie wished Ollenfrond wasn't such an eloquent speaker.

A boat was lowered over the side. Ollenfrond and Gangplank rowed off toward the dock as the crew of the newly christened Snow White Swan waved and cheered. No one on board was sure what Ollenfrond was going to do but they were confident that he would succeed.

Absolutely no shore leave was granted. Nastie was concerned enough about letting Gangplank out of his sight without having the added worry of other crew members wandering through town. He couldn't be sure their pirate urges wouldn't suddenly pop up and make them do something rash, like steal a lady's bonnet or rob a bank. If local authorities had to come to his ship to discuss a member of the crew's misbehavior they might recognize Nastie, even without his famous moustache. Then it would be curtains for the captain and crew of the Green Gouldred!

OLLENFROND AND THE BANKERS

While Nastie and his crew paced the decks trying to keep their greedy minds off the surrounding fat merchant ships, Ollenfrond and Gangplank arrived at the First National Bank of Seaworthy.

Ollenfrond informed the teller that he wished to discuss an investment of half a million pounds of gold with the head of the investment department. The amazed teller had never heard of such a large sum of money in his life. Somehow he managed to keep from fainting as he led the pair directly to the president's office.

Ollenfrond introduced himself and Gangplank as Mr. Frond and Mr. Plank, investment counselors of a client who wished to remain anonymous. Before long all the necessary arrangements were made. The bank president sent messengers to the captains of every ship in the harbor, inviting them to dinner. They all accepted because they had heard rumors about an incredible quantity of gold and suspected that the dinner might have something to do with it.

Everyone gobbled down the sumptuous banquet as quickly as possible so they could find out about the gold. Mr. Frond addressed the group. At first the ship captains thought that 'Mr. Frond's' proposal was preposterous. But, before the evening was over, all agreed to proceed.

Ollenfrond and Gangplank arrived back at the ship long after midnight, much too tired to speak to anyone. The crew began to grumble that they had a right to know what was happening to their money. Although he didn't even know what had happened himself, Captain Nastie assured the crew that everything was fine and they would hear about it in the morning. Ollenfrond hadn't said anything about telling anyone what had happened in the morning, but as far as Nastie was concerned that was precisely what Ollenfrond was going to do first thing before breakfast, whether he liked it or not. Nastie refused to wait any longer without a report.

By 5:30 the next morning the crew was gathered outside Ollenfrond's cabin. They weren't going to miss anything. At 7:00

Nastie himself arrived. At 7:01 Nastie ran out of patience and knocked on the door.

Ollenfrond stepped out onto the deck, stretching and yawning. He looked across the harbor full of boats.

"Lovely view," Ollenfrond said, smiling. "What do you think of it, Brute?"

Nastie looked at the ships only a super human effort on his part had prevented him from plundering. "Lovely," he said in irritated response.

"Isn't it nice to think that they are all yours?" asked Ollenfrond

"That is a nice thought," answered Nastie. "But I wish you would get down to business and tell me what you have done with my money."

"That's what I'm talking about," said Ollenfrond. "We bought the ships in the harbor. They are all yours."

"You didn't have enough money to buy all those ships," said Nastie, feeling his anger rise.

"True," answered Ollenfrond, "but our deposit was so large that the bank loaned us the rest of the money, half payable next year at this time and the rest due two years from now."

Nobody said a word. They stood there with their mouths hanging wide open and stared at the ships. It seemed impossible. But if Ollenfrond said they owned them they did and that was that. Smiles spread like measles. They broke into a spontaneous celebration that continued until the last pirate fell snoring on the deck.

All around them ships prepared for their new assignments. Ollenfrond and Nastie retired to the captain's cabin to discuss cargoes and destinations for each ship. In private Nastie asked some questions which were bothering him.

"What if we don't have enough money to cover the loan?" asked Nastie. "It is possible that since we now own so many ships we will only encounter our own ships as we sail in search of merchant vessels to plunder."

"But you won't plunder vessels any longer," explained Ollenfrond. "Have you forgotten that you bought those ships to work for you? From now on your profits will come from trade, not plunder. And those profits will easily cover the amount due on the loan."

"Of course," said Nastie, congratulating himself for having Ollenfrond as his business manager.

FINDING A SOLUTION

Countries throughout the world noticed a severe drop in their bird populations. The endless migration of birds to Bertie's kingdom was impossible to control. Bertie was about to swallow his pride and ask Fernwake for help dealing with so many birds when he overheard a little boy ask his mother what it had been like when birds lived above the ground.

"Was there room to run and play?" he asked, as he carefully watched the sidewalk to avoid stepping on three baby sparrows who had strayed from their mother.

"Things were different then," answered his mother. "Birds and people didn't live together at all. We had no laws in common. Birds actually spent their time watching out for people. They didn't depend on us for anything. They lived their own separate lives."

Bertie watched the child. In spite of his great love for birds, the young King felt sorry for him. When he was that boy's age there were no laws to prevent children from running because they might step on a bird by mistake. Complaints were becoming common at Bird Lovers Society meetings. Even Bertie was beginning to feel like there really were too many birds! He called a special session to discuss the problem of overcrowding.

"Maybe there is a way to design a separate community for birds," he suggested. He invited everyone to submit solutions.

Sketches, diagrams and letters poured in. Mrs. Merriwinkle, the fourth grade teacher, asked her class to draw pictures of what they thought the bird community should look like. She took all the drawings to King Bertie. He studied them very carefully. Some had interesting ideas he planned to show his architects.

The bottom drawing in the pile caught his attention. It was a detailed pencil sketch by Sparrow Featherbottom, the youngest girl in the class. As Bertie examined it his eyes grew wider and wider and the smile on his face grew broader and broader.

Sparrow had designed the perfect Bird Village. The drawing

showed Bertie's kingdom spreading in all directions with people happily walking, their eyes free to wander where they chose. Children were running and playing. There were very few birds on the ground. Floating above the kingdom was a tremendous nest covered with tiny houses and bushes and little berry trees where all the birds lived. The nest was held in place by twelve tremendous balloons which were anchored to the four corners of the kingdom by thick ropes.

It looked like a perfect solution. But it was so large he could see no way to build it. It occurred to Bertie that since Sparrow Featherbottom had designed the village she might also know how to build it. He invited her to share hot chocolate and chocolate-chip cookies with him the following afternoon.

Sparrow walked to the castle as soon as she got out of school. She was a little nervous about having a meeting with the King all by herself. But as soon as she was introduced to Bertie she knew it would be easy to be friends with him. They discovered that they both liked to fill their cups to the brim with marshmallows before pouring in the cocoa. Soon they were laughing and chatting as if they had known each other forever. Sparrow was pleased that Bertie liked her drawing. She hoped to be an architect when she was older.

"There is only one question I have about your design," said Bertie. "How would you build such a large structure?"

"That's easy enough," answered Sparrow. "I'd build it on the ocean."

"Like a huge raft?" asked Bertie, amazed at the simplicity of the idea.

"Exactly," said Sparrow. "It's the only place where there would be enough room, unless you chopped down hundreds of trees, and that would be a terrible thing to do."

"You're absolutely right!" said Bertie. "You have solved all our problems. We'll name it Featherbottom Village after you. We'll start work tomorrow. You shall be my personal advisor for the project. It will be up to you to okay all plans and drawings. I was going to say that you will be a great architect someday, but you already are one!"

Bertie and Sparrow shook hands and said goodbye, each of them was wishing it were already tomorrow so they could get started.

THE GREAT NEST

Never was a project built so quickly and with such enthusiasm. For the next four months, the birds and people worked in absolute harmony. At the end of that time, Featherbottom Village was complete. It was a work of art, worthy of being called one of the Wonders of the World.

Each house had been built to the scale of its bird occupant. A natural setting similar to where that particular bird normally lived had been created around his house. Stork homes had basements that looked like chimney tops. Eagle homes were built of stone and resembled rocky crags on mountaintops. Woodpecker homes were carved out of tree trunks. Ducks had tiny ponds in front of their houses. Pigeon houses were built on top of marble busts. Each bird had his own carefully designed takeoff and landing area.

There was a Main Street with shops, grocery stores, boutiques, banks, feather dressers and movie theaters. There were bird schools, bird churches, bird hospitals, bird police departments, bird fire departments and bird libraries. There was even a bird pet shop where trained fleas, flea dwellings and organic flea food were sold.

The birds wasted no time moving into their new homes. Curtains appeared in every window. Mats were placed at each front door. Lawns were mowed and flowers were planted. Living with people had obviously affected birds' lifestyles.

Meanwhile, the 12 balloons were carefully sewn out of blue and lavender silk. Thick hemp ropes were wound with silver and green cords. Huge iron rings were attached to mighty oak trees at each corner of the kingdom so the bird village could be anchored down.

With the birds living on the floating Nest, people could again walk around freely. Some were heard to say that there was no need to fly the bird village over the kingdom when it floated so nicely on the ocean. But the birds were adamant about wanting their village high in the air. It seemed like the most sensible place since the Nest made navigation in the harbor difficult.

The balloons and ropes were finished and attached to the Nest. Fires were built and the balloons were filled with hot air. The Nest rose slowly from the water. Soon it was high enough so it wouldn't bump into any rooftops in town. The people of the kingdom divided into four groups. Each group began to pull one of the ropes. Slowly the Nest sailed over the kingdom. The ropes were tied off at the four great oak trees. Featherbottom Village continued to rise higher and higher until the ropes were taut and the Nest could climb no more.

Everyone cheered. Sparrow Featherbottom's idea had worked. People danced in the streets. The birds held their own celebration in their new nest-home. Huge buckets of champagne and worms were consumed. Nobody even thought about going to sleep for five days.

"CATS ANONYMOUS"

The Secret Society of Cat Lovers gathered in Fernwake's private courtyard. From there, the Wizard, Timothy, Jonalon, Dr. Feather, Gray Malkin and Tuna-Una watched as the bird village was pulled over their heads. Like a dark cloud passing across the land, the incredible Nest erased the Sun. While it had floated on the ocean the Nest was beautiful, but from underneath the people could no longer see the tiny houses and miniature gardens. All they could see was the bottom of the Nest, which no one had ever even considered painting or decorating. A roof of tangled twigs now hung between them and the sky.

"How awful it is," said Timothy. "The people will soon protest so much that Bertie will have to get rid of it."

"If only that were the case," said Fernwake. "But see how they celebrate. The people are so happy to be able to dance and play again that it will be a long time before they notice the Sun is gone. They will look up at the sky to admire the wonderful Nest they all helped build. They are very proud of it. It takes a courageous man to find fault with his own handiwork."

Tuna-Una and Gray Malkin were expecting kittens. They were glad that they would soon be sharing a family. But they were extremely concerned about what the future held for their kittens. It was not right for them to be born in a land where they were not wanted. As he lay in the shadow of the Nest, Gray Malkin realized that he had to act soon if a solution was to be found in time.

That night he did something he had not done since cats had been banished. He went for a long walk through the countryside beyond the castle walls. In spite of the danger, he felt he had to get out. Since the Nest covered the Moon there was no light to bounce against the white patches of fur on his face and neck so he was nearly invisible.

He moved swiftly over country roads, as if he were in a race. His only opponent was time. There was no contest. Time would get to the end of the race no matter what Gray Malkin did. He sat down beside a tree to scratch his ear. The silence was broken by a loud sigh from the other side of the tree. Gray Malkin froze and listened. The sigh turned into a voice.

"How could I have forgotten the Sun when I designed that Nest?" asked the despairing voice. "What a terrible thing it is to be praised for a disaster. They don't even see what a mistake it is. How can people be so blind that they don't miss the Sun? Plants are so much more sensitive than people. The flowers in my mother's garden are already beginning to wilt from lack of sunlight."

Gray Malkin felt like walking around to the other side of the tree to comfort the unhappy voice, but it was a young voice so it probably belonged to a member of the Bird Lovers Society. Gray Malkin was afraid he might be captured and sent out of the country. The voice continued to talk.

"So much is wrong with the kingdom now, all because King Bertie hates cats. I wish the cats were home again. I don't care if I never see another bird as long as I live. If only that Nest would blow away."

Gray Malkin's ears perked up. All he had to do was figure out how to blow the Nest away. He was so grateful for the suggestion that he walked right around the tree and rubbed up against the little girl sitting there.

"Where did you come from?" Sparrow Featherbottom asked. Gray Malkin didn't say a word. He just purred and curled up on her lap. The two of them sat there in silence, watching the dark spot where the Moon was supposed to be.

PLANS AND PREPARATIONS

Gray Malkin called a special meeting of the Cat Lovers Society. He told them about the girl.

"How in the world could we blow that huge Nest away?" asked Timothy.

"Are you forgetting those thick ropes?" asked Jonalon.

"People would begin to wonder why we were standing around huffing and puffing," chuckled Dr. Feather, as he imagined how funny they would look. "We'd probably be at it for years,"

Tuna-Una put her paw on Gray Malkin's head to see if he had a fever. She had never heard him come up with such a ridiculous idea. Gray Malkin felt that the idea was not to be treated lightly. He turned to Fernwake for support. The Wizard had been staring at the Nest.

"What a fantastic idea!" said Fernwake. "The Nest can certainly be blown away. But we can't just blow it away and forget about it. We must consider its destination."

"You mean we have to figure out where it's going to land?" asked Jonalon. "That sounds even more impossible."

"How would you feel if an uninvited nest full of birds landed on top of your town?" asked Dr. Feather. "The Wizard is right. We can't just pass the problem on to someone else. We must solve it once and for all, though I can't imagine how."

"We can't blow the Nest away ourselves," said Fernwake. "But a powerful Storm could do it. Let's look at the globe to see which one to ask."

Everyone followed the Wizard to the tremendous globe in the corner of her study. The Wizard spun it around and around. For what seemed like forever there was no sound except the soft whirr of the globe. Fernwake's finger traced mysterious patterns over the face of the globe. After a while the group began to notice that her finger kept returning to the same spot. Finally she stepped back and smiled.

"What do you think of those islands?" she asked.

They all crowded around to examine a group of funny shaped dots near the equator. There didn't seem to be anything special about them.

"That," said Fernwake dramatically, "is where we shall send the Nest. The climate is warm. Food is abundant. Other islands are plentiful. The Nest would become just another island in the group. The birds could decide whether they wanted to stay there or migrate back to their original homes."

"According to my calculations," continued the Wizard, "an extremely powerful Southeast Storm would be able to carry the Nest there."

"But how will you talk to a Storm?" asked Timothy.

"When the next Southeast Storm blows through, I will plant a special offering of seeds in the courtyard. The Storm will not be able to resist the temptation to water the seeds. I will speak to it then. It will carry my request home to where the mighty Southeast Storm King dwells. We can only hope that he decides in our favor. Meanwhile we must find a way to weaken the ropes so the right Storm can carry it away."

"What a dreadful mistake it would be if the wrong Storm took it," said Dr. Feather.

From under a perfectly ordinary dinner napkin, Fernwake pulled a beautiful banana-nut cake. The Wizard announced that it was a contemplation cake and gave everyone a generous slice. No one said a word as they ate. They weren't sure a solution was possible and wasted several minutes contemplating the possibility that what they were trying to contemplate was impossible. Dr. Feather bit down hard on a bit of shell that had gotten into the cake by mistake.

"Someone should invent a nut that doesn't have a shell," he said, promising himself that he would bite into banana-nut cakes more carefully in the future.

"Birds love nuts," commented Jonalon.

"Our problem isn't nuts," said Timothy, irritated that her train of thought had been interrupted. "It's ropes! Maybe if birds ate ropes instead of nuts our problems would be solved."

"That's it!" cried Jonalon. "If we put nuts in the ropes, the birds will peck at the nuts and weaken the ropes."

"I wonder how many nuts we should put in the ropes so the birds weaken them the proper amount?" said Timothy.

"How will we get the nuts there in the first place?" asked Dr. Feather.

"I could climb the ropes on a foggy night and stick them in," suggested Gray Malkin, hoping the fog would be the same color as his fur. He was willing to do anything for his soon-to-be-born family.

"I'll make a suede nut bag for you to wear around your neck," said Jonalon.

"And I will figure out how many nuts are needed in each rope," said Timothy, who was already working on a long column of numbers on the back of a napkin.

"Well," said Dr. Feather, "I guess that leaves it up to Tuna-Una and me to decide which nuts the birds like best."

Everyone was glad that the Storm was the Wizard's responsibility. They all wondered how she was going to talk to the Southeast Storm. It sounded impossible to all of them, yet the Wizard did not look even slightly concerned.

Gray Malkin chaired their meeting the following afternoon. "Jonalon, can I wear the seed pouch around my waist?" he asked. "I think it would work more easily there than around my neck."

"Certainly," said Jonalon. "The pouch is ready. Let's measure your waist and I'll make a belt."

"Thank you," said Malkin. "Fernwake, can you carry me to the top of the ropes under the protection of your magic cape?"

"I wish I could," said Fernwake. "Unfortunately the cape is made a special way so that birds can detect it even though they can't see it. Otherwise I might cause serious mid-air collisions. But I will go with you and wait for you on the ground."

"The nuts will be at the Royal Nutter's Shop tomorrow morning," reported Dr. Feather.

Tuna-Una glanced nervously at Gray Malkin. Everything was happening so quickly. She was concerned about his safety. The new

Moon would bring three nights of darkness and she could smell a hint of dampness in the air that might create fog.

"It will be soon," she said softly. The faint stirrings of new life within her made her heart rise to her throat in fear.

"Let's consult the *Chinese Book of Changes* to determine whether this is an auspicious time," suggested the Wizard.

There was silence as Fernwake cast the yarrow stalks used to access the wisdom of the *Book of Changes*. The process yielded the symbol for 'Approach'. The meaning was clear. It was the correct and auspicious time for them to act. But with the possibility of success came the warning that all would be lost unless the evil was subdued before it had a chance to begin. They resolved that if evil ever became a problem, they would figure out how to eliminate it.

"Now we know we must proceed," said Fernwake. "I will speak to the Clouds tomorrow to see if they can be persuaded to blanket the kingdom in soft Fog."

That night no one could sleep, each kept awake by the conflict between the frustration of waiting and the fear of acting. To take her mind off her fears, Timothy embroidered as many symbols of luck, protection and good fortune as she could dream up on Gray Malkin's soft suede pouch. Jonalon brought Gray Malkin a sample piece of the rope that held the nest down. The gray cat spent hours practicing ways to stick nuts into it. Since nobody but Fernwake could think of anything else to do, they sat around watching Gray Malkin and offered suggestions which only made the poor cat more nervous.

Fernwake spent the afternoon studying ways to persuade Clouds to do one's bidding. As the Sun began to set she wrapped her magic cape over her shoulders and left without a word.

Three hours later she reappeared with thick Fog rolling in behind her. "We must begin immediately," she said, picking up Gray Malkin. Again she was gone without a word. Gray Malkin had questions to ask but since Fernwake said nothing Malkin felt he should follow the Wizard's example.

Suddenly they were at the first rope. Fernwake placed Gray Malkin on the ground, scratched him encouragingly under the chin and withdrew into her cape.

THE BRAVE CAT

Gray Malkin felt terribly alone as he looked up the first great rope. He could barely see a foot in front of his nose as he began to climb. Soon the rope seemed to lead to nowhere above and nowhere below. He shivered in the Fog and wished he were home by the fire. There were so many thoughts filling his mind that he reached the top much sooner than he expected. The knots on the pouch were stiff in the dampness. It seemed to the cat that it took longer to open the pouch than it had taken to climb the rope. He worked the nuts into the rope carefully and slid down.

Fernwake was not there! Afraid to waste time, Gray Malkin limped off toward the next rope, hoping that Fernwake would find him. He planted nuts in the second rope without difficulty and went on to the third. There was an odd stirring in the wind above him as he slid down the rope. But the sensation disappeared long before he reached the ground.

The hours passed quickly and he grew very tired. Soon Daylight would climb up over the mountains. The Sun would quickly follow and chase away the Fog. As he pulled himself up the last rope he wished with all his heart that Fernwake would appear. If it hadn't been for thoughts of his family, he would have given up to fear and loneliness.

As Gray Malkin wedged the nuts into the last rope he felt an odd stirring in the wind again. Suddenly there was a powerful rushing sensation in the air behind him. He turned in time to see a tremendous, dark- winged eagle soar by.

For a moment Gray Malkin wasn't sure if the bird had seen him. But his question was answered almost immediately. The eagle made a rapid turn and plummeted down, its beak and talons aimed directly at Gray Malkin's eyes.

The cat stared in horror at what appeared to be an unavoidable missile. He turned his head away and stuffed the last nuts into the rope. Even if he lost his life it was still possible that the eagle would not understand what he had been doing and the final plans could be completed without him.

The air behind him was filled with furious rushings. Gray Malkin turned quickly, his good front paw raised in defense. He struck out as he turned and caught something in his claws. Whatever it was seemed to rip away and, except for violent air currents, there was absolutely nothing there.

The eagle had disappeared so suddenly it was as if someone had dropped a velvet curtain between the cat and the bird. Gray Malkin examined his claws to see if anything remained of what he had momentarily caught. A small gray thread was wrapped around one claw, a thread from Fernwake's cape. The Wizard had saved him! He slid quickly down the rope. Even before he reached the ground he felt himself being scooped up in Fernwake's cape. It was the most wonderful sensation he had ever experienced. No fireside had ever felt so warm. No bowl of cream had ever been so soothing. He fell asleep under the Wizard's arm, secure in the knowledge that the night's ordeal was over.

When he woke up, Tuna-Una was curled around him and they were both on Fernwake's lap. The Wizard was relating their incredible adventure.

"I was barely able to thrust myself between Gray Malkin and the eagle," said Fernwake. "Then I spun the bird around in my cape and carried him to the opposite side of the Nest. When he regains his senses, his memory of tonight will be nothing more than of being caught in a whirlwind. The cat will have been forgotten. Our nuts are planted. The ropes will soon be weakened. We are committed to our goal."

The next morning Dr. Feather and Jonalon checked the ropes. Several small birds had already discovered the delicious nuts. Soon larger birds would investigate. Everything was proceeding as planned.

HOW TO FIND A STORM

Fernwake sat up all night reading a 14-volume *History of Weather* in an attempt to uncover a pattern in the actions of Southeast Storms. However, no pattern was specific enough to be helpful. A circle of rich soil was ready to receive the seeds which would notify the Storm that someone wished to consult it. The seeds could not be planted until the right Storm was nearly upon them so the tower was outfitted with the latest weather-sensing devices.

By the end of the week the little group was convinced they were experiencing the longest wait in the history of waiting. The ropes were definitely weakening. Fernwake was concerned that another Storm might soon carry the Nest away by mistake. If only a mild Southeaster would pass through she could explain their request and be confident that it would relay her message to the Storm Center. But days passed and her hopes diminished.

In the middle of the wait, four miraculous creatures, no bigger than field mice, were born to Tuna- Una and Gray Malkin. The first-born was one of those special cats that looks gray right-side-up and white upside-down, just like his father. The second and third were matching tabbies, exactly like Tuna-Una. The fourth was a solid black little girl whose voice, even at birth was the loudest in the group. Everyone was so excited that an entire day went by without anyone checking the ropes or weather instruments.

When they were five days old, the kittens opened their eyes. A whole new life began for them. Sometimes it seemed like there had to be at least ten kittens to cause as much trouble as those four little devils created.

The day the little black kitten, Ling-Pie, got tangled in Timothy's ball of yarn was not to be forgotten. Although it took no more than three minutes to untangle her, she screamed so loud it made the ordeal seem more like it took an hour. She figured out quickly that a little screaming resulted in hours of comforting and attention. Gray Malkin explained to her that the screaming was totally unnecessary. Unfortunately Ling-Pie didn't seem the least bit interested in reason. She had found a good thing and she wasn't going to give it up.

Gray Malkin called Fernwake to the courtyard. The instruments warned of the approach of wind and rain from the southeast. As they watched the Moon light up the edge of an advancing Southeast Cloudbank, a strong North Wind blew in.

Suddenly a terrific battle raged between the opposing Clouds and Winds. Thunder and Lightning crashed against the distant mountains for three hours before the Moon interfered and broke up the argument. The Moon forced the Southeast Clouds to withdraw and allowed the North Wind to continue along its original path.

The Clouds of the Southeast protested that the Moon's decision was totally unfair. The silent Moon continued to shine brightly at the edge of the kingdom. The Southeast Clouds finally withdrew to regroup, grumbling and thundering among themselves.

"Our Storm is retreating," cried Gray Malkin.

"Only for a little while," said Fernwake. "It is angry now and it will ask the Southeast Storm King to send help. The Moon may have turned it away this evening, but that Storm is determined to cross our territory."

"Will it be back soon?" asked Gray Malkin.

"Yes," answered Fernwake. "And when it returns it will have all the power it needs to wrench the Nest from its ropes. The Moon herself will not attempt to stop it. She will withdraw behind a Guardian Cloud."

"I had hoped for a gentle Storm," continued the Wizard. "If we are to succeed I must now face the wrath of the great and angry Southeast Storm King himself. There is no alternative. I fear mighty rains will wash away my pleas long before they reach the ear of such a powerful Storm. I must prepare myself."

"What will the Storm King do to you?" asked Gray Malkin fearfully.

Fernwake did not answer. She did not wish to share her fears with her friends. She withdrew to her study and remained there all the following day, seeing no one.

Gray Malkin told the others what had occurred. They were

extremely afraid of what might happen to Fernwake. Dr. Feather thought the entire idea should be abandoned to the fates rather than risk the Wizard's life. Everyone agreed and they went to Fernwake's study to tell her their decision.

The Wizard was sitting at her desk when they entered. Her hands were folded quietly and her eyes stared very hard, seemingly at nothing. "She appears to be in a trance," said Dr. Feather. The doctor tried to wake her without success. He turned away, shaking his head.

"There is nothing we can do," said the doctor sadly. "Her mind has left her body to be near the coming Storm. She must gather more power within herself than she has ever called together in all her time on Earth. The spirits in this room are crowded by our presence. We must leave her alone. May the Fates respect her will."

Everyone left the study except Gray Malkin, who crouched under the Wizard's chair and hoped that he was not taking up too much room.

THE SOUTHEAST STORM

The great Thunderhead Clouds of the Southeast Storm gathered in the afternoon. The setting Sun turned them into pink and gold mountains. People looked out from under the Nest to admire their beauty. They barely heard the warning of the town crier who walked through the streets calling, "A terrible Storm will pass over us tonight. Fasten your shutters and lock your doors! Put buckets under your leaks and chimneys on your candles!"

Sunset was the one time during the day when the townspeople got to see the Sun as it sank below the Nest and they didn't want to miss it just because someone told them to close their shutters. What damage could the Storm do as long as they were under the protective Nest?

Timothy, Dr. Feather and Jonalon stood in the Wizard's courtyard, watching the Clouds, too. "We could lock Fernwake in her study," suggested Jonalon.

"That would be impossible," the doctor reminded Jonalon. "We cannot interfere in any way. She must do what she has decided to do."

The Sun sank away to more friendly skies. The Moon peeked from behind a Cloud but retreated when she saw the gathering Storm.

The Clouds began their rain dance. They threw themselves into each other, sending thunderous warnings of their power rolling across the countryside. Lightning flashed its authority and children hid under their beds. A clap of Thunder like a pistol shot sounded in the valley and before its echo had died, the Southeast Storm fell upon the kingdom. The Nest would provide no protection tonight. The Storm King himself had arrived.

Fernwake walked calmly into the courtyard and stepped into the circle of earth. She ceremoniously sprinkled a ring of seeds around herself. As rain began to fall she noticed Dr. Feather, Timothy, Jonalon, Gray Malkin, Tuna-Una and the four kittens crowded at the window. She left the circle and closed the shutters so they could not see. Then she stepped back inside the circle and raised her arms high into the now pouring rain.

Lightning shot upward from her outstretched fingers. She clapped her hands together and the sound they made was Thunder. She opened her mouth and commanded the Southeast Storm

Winds to carry her words. No man heard her call. Her voice was Wind. But still the sounds rose, albeit weakly, to reach the Storm King's ear.

In response he sent a drowning rain to wash away the strange vibrations that were trying to interrupt his work. A torrent of water streamed down to cover the Wizard's plea, but some of the drops found the circle of seeds. They rode back upward on rising currents of air.

"There is a ring of seeds below," they called, splashing into the Storm King's ear. He grumbled that he didn't wish to be bothered, but he couldn't resist checking the seeds. He was startled to see Lightning flash up from within the seed ring. He clapped a thunderous question down upon the Wizard to see what creature beside himself and his brothers had the power to create Lightning. The Thunder shook every house in the kingdom, but Fernwake remained strong.

"I am a soul who storms against man's interference with Nature," thundered the Wizard. "But my storming is weaker than the morning mist. I call upon you, oh Great One, to shower us with justice."

The Southeast Storm decided to send a Messenger Wind down to deal with Fernwake. It would have swept anyone away who didn't stand within a protective circle of gentle seeds. Every candle in the kingdom was blown out and shutters that had been slamming open and shut in a terrible racket were closed once and for all.

Fernwake stood completely still. She said nothing, for one does not speak words to the Wind. The Wizard's robes whipped around her and she felt herself being lifted off the ground as the Messenger Wind blew through her body, seeking the truth. Fernwake felt cool and empty and open when the Wind had gone.

Incredibly, the Storm King stopped to hear the Wizard's plea. Only a gentle rain continued its business of watering the kingdom.

During the dark stillness the tiny black kitten, Ling-Pie, slipped out the door of the Wizard's chambers. It had blown open when the Messenger Wind had visited, and now she scrambled up the wall to watch the Wizard. Just at that moment the Storm rolled out a giant clap of Thunder, knocking dishes off the shelves in every kitchen and sending Ling-Pie tumbling down the circular staircase. Before she could stop herself she was blown through the black walnut door at the bottom of the stairs. A new and more terrible Wind slammed the great door shut behind her.

She opened her little mouth as wide as she could and screamed. Yet nobody came running to her rescue. Ling-Pie closed her mouth in amazement. Not only was she all alone, but she was in a totally unfamiliar place. Somewhere far above Thunder crashed and Lightning transformed the hall where she sat into a flickering blue tunnel. Ling-Pie picked herself up and scampered off in search of help.

Thunder bounced and rumbled until each stone in the castle walls shook separately. The terrible Storm was laughing at the Wizard's request.

"Man has acted against Nature. Why should he be spared a punishment he so justly deserves?" rumbled the great Southeast Storm King. "It is time he learns what can result from upsetting the balance of living creatures which Nature spent so many millions of years establishing."

The Wizard felt a chill run through her and the Lightning flashes sputtered at her fingertips. "Escape while you can, poor wizard," boomed the Storm King. "Leave men to their fate. Your plea does not move me." The Storm King scornfully sent a bolt of Lightning crashing at the Wizard's feet to signify that he could strike the Wizard from the earth if he chose to do so.

Gathering strength from the Winds that filled her lungs, the Wizard clapped her hands in a thunderous rejection of the Storm King's decision. "To intentionally bring suffering on those who respect Nature would be as cruel as man's most irresponsible act," roared the Wind in the Wizard's voice.

The Messenger Wind felt the Wizard was right and added its own strength to Fernwake's voice. Its extra power carried Fernwake's words crashing directly into the ear of the Storm King.

"I shall not do your bidding!" howled the Storm King, sending ten bolts of Lightning straight toward the Wizard's head. The circle of seeds saved her life.

"You shall!" commanded the Wizard in a voice greater than a season of hurricanes.

"The trees and grasses and animals are my responsibility," screeched the Storm King, now swirling like a tornado. "Man is responsible for himself!"

"Who gave you the right to destroy something which you have the power to save?" cried Fernwake. Her question crashed against mountains and bounded and rebounded to ring in the Storm King's ear.

Even the Wizard was startled by the strength of the sounds she uttered. They seemed to have more power than the voice of the Storm King himself, who quickly realized that many of the Winds had been won over by the Wizard's pleas. One by one they were deserting him to help the Wizard's cause. If he lost any more strength, the Moon would come out and crush him into nothing more than a babbling brook. He did not intend to suffer such humiliation.

"There is merit in your words, Wizard of the Winds," rumbled the Southeast Storm King. "It is lucky for you that I have the power to restore the balance of Nature. Although I obviously need no assistance, I would be willing to hear your plans."

"The ropes which hold the Great Nest have been weakened," explained the Wizard.

"Any Storm could tear that nest from its ropes." mumbled the Southeast Storm. "Why do you bother me with such an insignificant problem?"

"It is our great good fortune that you are here," answered Fernwake. "The ropes will be like straws to you, Great Storm King. But tremendous strength tempered with gentleness is needed to carry the Nest far away and place it unharmed in a more appropriate location. We could not make such a request of any careless passing Storm with little purpose in life other than to drive people indoors."

"I assume you selected a location which is not out of my way," continued the Storm.

"Far to the southeast and just beneath the equator lie the

Tumbleweed Islands, not far from the Canary Islands," said Fernwake, making her voice sound as tempting as a summer breeze.

"A fair splattering of friendly islands," interrupted a much-subdued Storm, "and an excellent place for birds. Precisely the spot I had in mind"

"Then you will help us?" asked Fernwake.

"Certainly!" answered the Storm King with a happy clap of Thunder for emphasis.

"Is there anything we can do for you in return?" asked the Wizard.

"Yes," came the quick reply. "Don't tell anyone it wasn't my idea."

And with that, the Storm King summoned all its Winds to join in the new project. They took off toward the Nest, thundering and cavorting like a herd of children out celebrating the Fourth of July with the world's noisiest fireworks.

The weakened ropes held longer than anyone had expected. The winds pushed and pulled with all their strength. Thunder shook the trees to their roots. Lightning flashed against the knots. Still they held with the tenacity of a two-year-old who doesn't want to share. The Storm King decided that the only way to take the Nest was to concentrate on breaking one rope at a time.

With all its force unleashed against a single rope the problems were eliminated. Each rope in turn snapped like a thread. Then, with one enormous farewell roar, the Southeast Storm moved on, carrying the Nest and the night with it.

Like champagne out of a bottle, sunshine burst across the countryside. People ran from their houses and stood staring up into the clear freedom of the skies. No one knew what to say. They were afraid to admit they were glad the Nest was gone. One little girl who felt that her voice wasn't loud enough to shout her joy ran to the top of the bell tower and pulled the ropes as hard as she could.

As the bells sounded, people everywhere began to cheer and dance. Garlands were hung across the narrow streets. Everyone left all chores and responsibilities behind to celebrate the wonder of uninterrupted sunshine and open sky.

THE SUN

Tuna-Una turned away from the spectacle at the window and discovered that Ling Pie was missing. As she nosed around dark corners she picked up a Ling-Pie scent that led under the great door. She immediately called for help. Dr. Feather remained behind to take care of the rest of the kittens.

Down the stairs the searchers ran, hoping to find Ling-Pie safe and sound at the bottom. But she wasn't there. Somehow she had gotten through the heavy walnut door, too. Gray Malkin and Tuna-Una felt fear rising in their throats. Their kitten was lost in enemy territory. They opened the door and stalked cautiously down the hall.

By that time Ling-Pie was far away in another corner of the castle. Exhausted from looking for help, she found a chair full of very soft cushions, burrowed into them and fell fast asleep.

Bertie was awakened that morning by the sound of bells ringing from all corners of the kingdom. Outside his door his ministers were drawing straws to see who would deliver the terrible news.

The young King stared at the beautiful sky in all its sparkling glory. It took a moment for him to remember what was different about the view. A gentle knock at his door brought his mind back to reality and he saw immediately what was missing.

"Come in," he shouted. In his haste and anger he buttoned his shirt wrong twice and ran from his room toward the courtroom without bothering to speak to anyone.

The ministers followed Bertie, their robes billowing behind them. They kept glancing back and forth at each other, wondering what to do. Not only was the Nest nowhere to be found, but the entire kingdom had begun a spontaneous celebration. There were sure to be serious reprisals against such a terrible uprising.

Bertie swept into the courtroom and plopped himself down on the throne. A blood-curdling screech filled the room. Bertie jumped to his feet and turned around to look at his throne. There, standing on top of the pillows with her back arched indignantly and her mouth open in a furious hiss, was Ling-Pie. She was no bigger than a teacup, but the anger she so vehemently expressed could not have been made clearer by sounding off all the cannons in the Royal Navy.

She was merely announcing that Bertie had almost sat on her tail. But how was poor Bertie to understand? Judging from the way she was carrying on, he was sure he had nearly killed her.

One of the ministers rushed forward. "I shall dispose of that ferocious cat immediately," he said, reaching toward Ling-Pie.

Just then Tuna-Una, Gray Malkin and the Wizard arrived at the courtroom door. Tuna-Una was about to spring forward and attack everyone in the room in an attempt to rescue her baby but the Wizard stopped her.

"No! You shall not touch the kitten," said Bertie, restraining his minister. "She is truly the bravest child I have ever encountered. Please go instead to the kitchen and fetch a bowl of cream."

Tuna-Una and Gray Malkin ducked behind the Wizard as the man raced out on his errand. They all peeked around the door to see what would happen next. By then Timothy and Jonalon had joined them.

"Tell me, young Princess," said Bertie addressing a somewhat calmer Ling-Pie, "What brings you to my throne so early in the morning?"

Ling-Pie let out one of her ear-splitting screams in answer.

"I see," said Bertie. "It is understandable that since you were lost in the terrible Storm you sought shelter in the most comfortable pile of pillows you could find."

Tuna-Una turned to Gray Malkin. "How did he understand what Ling-Pie was saying?" she asked in amazement.

Gray Malkin shook his head. He was equally surprised. The Wizard whispered something about the possibility that it might be because they were both spoiled children. Tuna-Una was too busy watching Ling-Pie and Bertie to notice what Fernwake had said.

Bertie offered Ling-Pie his hand. At first she withdrew into the pillows. But when she realized he was not making a threat she emerged and allowed him to rub between her ears. He placed the saucer of cream on the pillow beside her. When she finished her cream, she allowed Bertie to pick her up and hold her in his hand.

He lifted her gently to his face and was startled to hear the sound of a motor running at full throttle. "She isn't real," he said to his counselors. "She has a motor inside." Bertie was so disappointed he started to drop the kitten.

"Stop!" called Fernwake, rushing to the front of the room. "Don't drop her. She is as alive as you are. Sometimes it is impossible to believe how little you know about cats."

"Listen to that motor," said Bertie, holding Ling-Pie out toward the Wizard. "She is a toy!"

"That 'motor' is called a purr," explained Fernwake. "Cats purr when they are content. She is telling you she likes you very much, though I can't imagine why."

Bertie curled his tongue up in his mouth and tried to imitate the purring sound to let the kitten know that he liked her too. Ling-Pie smiled at him and continued to purr.

"Your Majesty," interrupted one of the counselors, "do you wish to discuss the birds?"

"Absolutely!" answered Bertie. "But I believe the cats should be the first matter of business this morning. Their problem has been ignored too long. Summon the royal trumpeters."

Seven royal trumpeters appeared almost immediately, dressed in silver and green heraldic costumes. They carried golden trumpets which were traditionally twice as long as the tallest man in the kingdom.

"Call my people together from every corner of the kingdom," commanded King Bertie, "with the sounds of good news."

The trumpeters hastened to do his bidding. It took little time for the people who were already celebrating in the streets to congregate beneath the King's balcony. They were all dressed in party colors and many carried baskets of flowers. A boy scaled the wall and draped the balcony with garlands. Throughout the crowd, happy sounds of flutes and harmonicas could be heard.

When Bertie appeared, the crowd cheered. He held out his hand. There was a frightened gasp. Silence filled in all the spaces. On Bertie's hand sat Ling-Pie. The crowd knew only too well how Bertie felt about cats and each heart feared for the tiny kitten's life.

"I hold before you a stowaway kitten, the child of renegade parents who stayed within the castle walls contrary to my edict," said Bertie. "This very morning I found her sleeping on my throne. Before I had a chance to throw her into the depths of the darkest dungeon she turned upon me, hissing and howling, fighting for the right to sleep undisturbed in a place of her own choosing."

"You have been called together as witnesses. I hereby proclaim and defend the right of every cat to sleep where he or she chooses. Ships will be made available immediately to return unfortunately banished cats to their own hearth sides. That concludes the first order of business today."

"The second concerns the whereabouts of our beautiful Nest and all the birds who were in the Nest during the Storm. The Wizard Fernwake explained that the Nest is now in the capable hands of the Southeast Storm Winds. It is being transported to a new and far more appropriate location in the Tumbleweed Islands. I am sure that I speak for all assembled here in wishing the Nest godspeed on its journey."

The crowd burst into cheers and song. People rushed off to retrieve their beloved cats.

Suddenly a warning signal flashed toward the castle from the lighthouse in the harbor. Such a signal had not been sent in thirty-three-and-a-third years. Many, including the sixteen-year- old King Bertie, had never seen one. A telescope was passed up from the crowd to Bertie.

The young King scanned the horizon until he sighted the unmistakable sails of the terrible Green Gouldred. Fear shivered its way through the crowd. As the ship sailed closer, Bertie could see golden banners gaily streaming from the masts. It was a curious way for a warlike pirate galleon to approach a harbor rich in plunderable goods. Behind the Green Gouldred more ships appeared, and more and more until the harbor was filled with an entire pirate navy.

No one knew what to think. The royal admiral assured Bertie that his men would do their best but that they didn't have much hope against so many obviously well-armed pirate ships. There was nothing anyone could do except stand there, staring silently at the advancing ships. The stillness hung like heavy blankets, blocking all motion.

WHAT NEXT?

A clear golden sound skittered across the water from the Green Gouldred. It rang warmly in every ear. It was not the objectionable sound of war at all. It was a song at first unfamiliar and yet somehow familiar, like a freshly remembered memory. Those at the shore with flutes and harmonicas began to pick out the tune, softly searching for notes. Timothy discovered tears rolling down her cheeks. She glanced around and saw others crying also.

"That was our father's song," she said quietly.

Bertie nodded. A whispering voice carried the message through the crowd. Hearts returned to visit the memory of the good King and his beloved Queen who had disappeared so many years ago. Fear of the advancing pirates was swallowed up in sad recollections.

The silence was broken when one of the royal counselors became hysterical. "We are about to be attacked by an ocean-full of pirates!" he shouted, "Why are we all standing around crying? We must defend ourselves!"

Bertie nodded. "You are absolutely right," he said calmly. A solution to the problem didn't seem to exist, even in the furthest corners of his mind. He turned to Fernwake, but the Wizard shook her head. She could think of nothing either. Suddenly Bertie had an idea.

"The pirates have us greatly out-numbered," he called out to the crowd, "They have the power to take whatever they wish. To stand against them would be a minor delay and we would suffer for our foolishness. Instead of arming ourselves, let us welcome them in peace," he continued. "If we surprise them with kindness we may gain some bargaining power. At the very least we will save lives."

Many grumbled that the idea sounded foolish and rash, but more saw wisdom in the young King's words. They gathered closer to hear his recommendations.

"Deck the harbor with the garlands you have gathered," Bertie directed, determined to sound brave and confident. "Set tables at the waterfront with all the fruits, wines, cakes and honeys to be found. Musicians, please come together and prepare a song of welcome."

"I will present Captain Nastie with a bouquet of flowers when he lands," offered Timothy, ready to do what she could to make the dreaded pirate captain feel welcome.

Everyone scattered, happy to have something to do besides fear the approaching pirates. By the time tiny figures could be seen on the decks of the Green Gouldred, everything was ready. Some of the people on the shore were convinced that people on the ships were waving to them.

A boat was lowered from the side of the Green Gouldred. A girl in the crowd who had been a lady-in-waiting to the long-lost Queen Tindra insisted that the woman in the rowboat was surely the missing Queen.

The sense of excitement in the crowd grew as the little boat drew near. The man and woman in the back of the boat really did look like the missing King and Queen. People began wading out into the water to meet them.

With great shouts and cheers they pulled the boat onto the sand and helped King Ollenfrond and Queen Tindra ashore. In the joy and confusion the pirates really were forgotten.

Timothy ran to her mother and threw her arms around her, dropping the bouquet intended for Brute Nastie. It tumbled along the ground until it landed at the pirate captain's feet. He plucked a pink rosebud from it and tucked the flower in among his blond curls. In their joy at seeing Ollenfrond and Tindra alive the townspeople were hugging everyone, including Nastie and Gangplank, who were quite embarrassed by all the affection.

Finally Brute glared down at a little man who was shaking his hand and said, "I happen to be the most ferocious pirate that ever forced a landlubber like you to walk the plank and I am hungry. If you don't bring me the biggest platter of smoked finnan haddie in the world within minus four seconds I will eat your children."

The little man scampered off in a terrible fright to find some finnan haddie. Nastie smiled and thought happily about the forthcoming treat. He forgot to be embarrassed and started looking for pretty girls to hug.

Hundreds of rowboats poured in from the ships in the harbor. Soon everyone was eating fruit and honeyed cakes and drinking sparkling juices and wines.

The threat of the pirates had completely vanished although nobody really knew where it went. Bits of conversation could be picked out above the general noise of the celebration like, "So you used to be a pirate....I must tell you about the time we surrounded the entire fleet of King Forkinhand...I'd like to be a pirate when I grow up....Has it really been that long since you made someone walk the plank?....Our King?.....Working for a pirate?....You must be joking....Best friends? ....I never knew a pirate could be so handsome....What brings you to our fair city?...and much more, mostly on the same subjects.

Brute Nastie walked among the people, happily eating finnan haddie with his fingers, nodding to everyone and smiling. He finally made his way to where Ollenfrond and Tindra were sitting with Bertie and Timothy. "So I see your family always throws parties when pirate ships approach, eh Ollie?" he asked Ollenfrond between bites.

"It certainly looks that way," laughed Ollenfrond."Let me introduce my children. Bertram and Timothy, meet Brute Nastie, captain of the greatest merchant fleet to sail the seven seas!"

"Thanks to your father," said Nastie modestly.

"I should say not," said Ollenfrond. "We did it together. And a fine job it was!"

"And will continue to be," added Nastie.

"I thought you were the richest pirate captain in the entire world," said Timothy.

"I used to be, my dear," Nastie answered, curling his moustache, "Now I am the richest merchant ship owner in the entire world. That is a hundred times better than being the world's richest pirate captain because I make a hundred times as much money and it is all legal!"

"How does that add up to being one hundred times as good?" asked Timothy, since she was always interested in a new math equation.

"You'll have to ask my business manager," said Nastie, polishing off his finnan haddie and nodding toward Ollenfrond.

"It was rather startling to be captured by pirates," said Tindra, "But once we adjusted to our new situation it really turned out to be fun."

"Mother!" cried Timothy. "How can you say such a thing?"

"How can you question me when you haven't tried it yet?" asked Tindra.

"Have you enjoyed being King?" Ollenfrond asked Bertie.

"It has been an incredible experience," answered his son.

"The kingdom certainly appears to be in fine shape," said Ollenfrond."Perhaps I should leave it in your capable hands."

"Not just yet," answered Bertie quickly. "I am ready for a long vacation right now."

"You might try an ocean voyage," suggested Ollenfrond, "Brute could teach you all about foreign trade."

A loud scream came from under the table. Ling Pie had given up trying to get Bertie's attention by rubbing against his ankle. Bertie leaned over and picked her up.

"I never thought I'd live to see the day when you had a kind thought for a cat," said Ollenfrond in surprise.

"This young Princess is the daughter of your old friend, Gray Malkin," said Bertie.

"That still doesn't explain it," commented Ollenfrond.

"It will take weeks to do that," answered Bertie. "I would love to go to sea with Captain Nastie as long as Ling-Pie can come, too, if she would honor me with her company. Also, there is one official act which I would like to perform before I return the crown to you."

"Certainly," said Ollenfrond.

Bertie signaled for the trumpets to sound and whispered something in Ling-Pie's ear. She scampered away. Everyone gathered around.

The kitten returned quickly, followed by her entire family. Gray Malkin and Tuna-Una were nervous. They still weren't sure they could trust Bertie.

Bertie stood up and drew his sword. "Come forward, Gray Malkin," commanded King Bertram.

Gray Malkin glanced at the Wizard to see what she thought about the situation. Fernwake nodded encouragingly. Gray Malkin swallowed and limped forward.

"Before all the world and especially to you I apologize for my unjust and unforgivable treatment of cats," said Bertie. "Nothing I can do will make up for what I have done. Nor will I ever be able to truly repay you for what you have done for us. Forever more my home is your home. And now I, King Bertram The First, confer upon you, Gray Malkin, the honor of Knighthood."

Bertie tapped Gray Malkin gently on the shoulder with his sword.

"Henceforth you shall be called Gray Malkin, Sir Stutterfoote," said Bertie, tying a royal ribbon around Gray Malkin's neck. From the ribbon hung a golden cat's head with sparkling emerald eyes.

Loud cheers rose like a fountain. Even the birds that had not been blown away with the Nest sang happily. Joy reached out from every heart to tie the kingdom together.

Once again, Nature ruled. All was well.

SPECIAL INFORMATION!

FREE GIFTS:
CAT and BIRD Yarn Craft projects for readers of
THE SINGLE-MINDED PRINCE!

Would you like a **FREE** copy of a needlepoint pattern of **Gray Malkin** or a crocheted **Bird** pattern like the bird on the cover of *THE SINGLE-MINDED PRINCE?* Please go to my website, www.CarrieStaples.com. You'll also find the **Mini-Monster Friend** pattern, an extra-easy project for kids of all ages. The patterns are from *THE YARN ANIMAL BOOK,* a craft book I wrote that was published by Simon and Schuster and became a Book of the Month Club Primary Selection.

Based on many years of requests we are about to re-publish *THE YARN ANIMAL BOOK.* Check my website, www.CarrieStaples.com, to find out about that book and my other publishing adventures like:

BOOKS IN PROGRESS:
HOW TO DRAW DEAD BUGS and
MOMMY JOURNALING

We need volunteers to draw dead bugs. Would you like to help? You'll get a credit if your drawings are used. Please email me at Carrie@CarrieStaples.com to volunteer and to be notified when my new books like *How to Draw Dead Bugs* will be available. Check my website, www.CarrieStaples.com, to find other projects that need your help like my book on art journaling for moms and dads who want to capture all the precious moments of childhood.

NATURE & ART JOURNALING

Check my website blog for drawings, writing
and photos from my daily journals.

ANOTHER FREE GIFT:

HELP!
Please look at the cover of *THE SINGLE-MINDED PRINCE* .
Tell me what **YOU** think the white spots on the worm heads are!

Email your ideas to <u>Carrie@CarrieStaples.com</u> and
we'll send you a **special coloring book page** based on
THE SINGLE-MINDED PRINCE plus I'll share some of the
amazing things other people thought the white spots were.

Thank you so much for supporting my work! I am grateful to have
wonderful readers like you! **I would love to hear from you so
I can thank you personally!**

Carrie Staples